The Last Wight Witch

Sarah Sprules

Books also by Sarah Sprules

Historical Fiction
Knighton Gorges: The Curse of Thomas Becket

Asperger's Syndrome/Autism/PDA
Looking at stars at three in the morning

As always I'd like to thank my wonderful family for all their love and support. I'd also like to take the opportunity to say thank you to my very dear friends Angela Hazell and Marie Bowden for all the fun and laughs and to Sarah Beck for being there, for nearly thirty years.

Prologue

Bembridge, Isle of Wight, 1808

The unrelenting summer sun beat down upon the bowed heads of the workers, transforming the fields of wheat into a veritable sea of gold for as far as the eye could see. Birds wheeled high overhead searching for cooler air, but there was only a very slight breeze rippling its way across the island, despite the close proximity to the open water. Every inhabitant from the village of Bembridge, who could stand unaided, had turned out for another day of backbreaking work, helping their neighbours to gather in the harvest. As they had each day, for nigh on two whole weeks and would happily return to do so the following year.

The men in the very first row with their long sharp bladed scythes hacked relentlessly at the tall shafts of the wheat, as they moved continuously forwards, followed closely by the young men with their curved sickles. The piles of fallen golden wheat were bundled together and tied into sheaves, and then the women and their children were the last to make up the group, picking up the leasings, the pieces that were too small to be taken in with the harvest. These insignificant leftover pieces were the women's assurance that despite the impending hard winter, their families would have enough bread to eat, if nothing else. Old Farmer Curtis kept a careful eye on the men, he was all too aware that if he didn't make his presence felt, they would deliberately cut the wheat too short and their wives following behind, would take a large majority of his crop home with them and he had no wish to be cheated out of precious wheat.

Phoebe Downer wiped the slick sheen of sweat from her brow and massaged the muscles in her lower back with fingers that were painfully stiff from constantly grabbing at the leasings, before anyone else could steal her share. In the year that had passed since she had last turned out to help with the harvest, she found that she had forgotten just how hard the work could be and made a note to remind herself of the fact, when she volunteered to do it all over again. Phoebe wasn't used to toiling in the fields all day and at harvest time; she was reminded of how thankful she was that her family were wealthy and it wasn't a way of life for them. Unlike the other labourers who were all hard at work, for Phoebe the back breaking toil was an escape from the day to day monotony of being stranded at home with her mother. For those around her, it was a desperate necessity to fend off starvation that drove them on and she saw at first hand, how hard the families worked just to claim the smallest of scraps.

Her mother despised her daughter's friendship with the local girls from Brading and Bembridge. She resented the fact that her only daughter spent her time running around the fields with her wanton friends, rather than indulging in more genteel pursuits. Several times a day, her mother would announce that a young lady should sit quietly embroidering or consumer herself with charitable deeds, not scamper around like a heathen, but Phoebe refused to listen. She was secretly annoyed by her mother's reluctance to remember where she herself had come from and found it hard to respect her parents and their high minded morals.

The Downer family had amassed their immense wealth through working closely with smugglers and benefiting from the considerable risks of many others. Several of the men they had sent over to France, had been impressed into the navy for five long years when caught by the loathed revenue cutters. Whilst her mother enjoyed the social standing that their wealth brought them, it was her father who was the shrewd man of business and took nothing for granted. He had always prided himself on spreading the risk, for every ship that got caught another ten had been successful and the family's finances had prospered to the point where they had begun to invest in more legitimate and less risky ventures, such as land and property.

Her mother's distinct disapproval of her friends was one of the main reasons that Phoebe put herself through the backbreaking labour of harvesting, as well as the chance to escape the claustrophobic confines of her home. Another reason was the celebratory feast that always happened when the last of the sheaves had been gathered safely in and the work was finally over. It was hard to believe that winter, was fast coming upon them, when the sun still shone so strongly and bees hummed lazily by in the heat. "Summer cannot last forever, the dark nights are never far behind," one of the old women had sighed wearily, whilst grabbing at the leasings and Phoebe had felt a shudder of foreboding run through her. The older women of the village were always full of stories and ancient sayings and whilst they worked, Phoebe thought they looked absurd with their white coifs, tied securely under their chins, though she privately cursed herself for not having thought to bring anything that would keep the sun from her neck. To cheer herself, she thought of the celebration they would have come nightfall. The food and drink were always so plentiful, that the hard physical labour was soon forgotten and she planned on eating until she couldn't touch another bite. Farmer Curtis was famous for his benevolence and generosity, for those who worked an honest day for him and Phoebe planned on availing herself of his generosity as much as possible.

She had never considered herself squeamish, but nonetheless it still made her jump whenever a mouse or tiny vole suddenly darted out from underneath the heaps of wheat and ran over her shoes, desperate to find another hiding place. From the crack of dawn, the men had kept up their singing, which helped to make the time go faster, distracting them from the monotony of the day ahead, but she noticed that their voices were cracking, as their throats dried up in the blistering heat. "Here y'are Phoebe" said Emily making her jump and passed her a small brown bottle of ale which she guzzled thirstily. "Thanks" she wiped her lips with the back of her hand and passed it along the line to Minnie, whose face was as red as a ripened tomato. "I'm so glad it's the last day. Even provoking my mother is not worth the pain anymore." Minnie laughed in agreement; she also belonged to a wealthy family, though their good standing could be traced back for generations unlike Phoebe's.

Phoebe and Minnie both lived in Brading, they had met Emily one market day, when she had made the arduous journey over from Bembridge and the three of them had been firm friends ever since. Emily's family wasn't as wealthy as theirs, so every year they came to the harvest to help her gather some wheat. Neither Phoebe nor Minnie minded helping their friend, they enjoyed the freedom; the chance to gossip, but most importantly, the harvest banquet was the most exciting night of the year and this year was sure to be the best one ever. Their parents had reluctantly agreed that the girls could spend the night at Emily's house, until they could safely travel back to Brading, on the understanding that Minnie's older brother would act as their chaperone.

Dragonflies hummed sluggishly along in the heat of the day and as soon as it was noon, Farmer Curtis sent a message down through the ranks that it was time for a break and the exhausted men, women and children all collapsed onto the ground as one. Each of the workers huddled together, trying to find what modest shade a wheat sheaf could offer and took their fill of much needed ale and succulent cuts of cold beef, along with several piles of freshly baked loaves and fresh vegetables. Farmer Curtis' wife had provided them with the best from her own table, she knew from experience that if the helpers were not kept well fed, then the harvest would take longer to get in and they were all eager to see it finished, before the weather changed and the rain came. Once the food had been devoured, the men produced long clay pipes, pushed their hats over their eyes, stretched their legs in front of them and began to doze contentedly.

"I am hoping to dance with my future husband tonight" boasted Emily, lying on her back, her black hair spread out haphazardly around her and one arm slung casually over her eyes, a shaft of yellow wheat hanging out of the side of her mouth. "Oh yes ? And do you have anyone in particular already in mind ?" Queried Minnie, a petite girl with dull brown hair and small green eyes which perpetually seemed to be dwarfed by her overly large, hooked nose. "No!" She declared indignantly. "That is the fun of the harvest feast after all. You get to try a few delights before you choose the one that you want to eat." Scandalised, the girls all fell about laughing, neither one of them in any doubt as to whether she was joking or not. "Emily I swear any man, who ends up with you, will find himself lumbered with a lifetime of trouble." Phoebe winked good naturedly at her friend "and a wife with the worst reputation in the whole of Bembridge into the bargain," chimed in Minnie and they all began to giggle once more. Emily placed her hat over her face and pretended to ignore them, too tired to argue after a long morning of gruelling work in the oppressive heat.

All too soon, the call went up that the break was over and the work began again in earnest. The atmosphere was far more jovial, once the workers had filled their stomachs and downed as much ale as they could manage. They knew that their efforts were almost at an end, the hottest part of the day had passed and the time to celebrate was nearly upon them. The islanders had been blessed with another bountiful harvest and the evening feast was sure to be one of the most splendid in some years. Every person toiling with sweat running down their backs in uncomfortable rivers, each had their minds firmly fixed on the evening ahead of them.

At the end of each day of harvesting, Phoebe and Minnie had happily handed over their leasings to Emily to take back to her cottage with her. Emily's father worked as a stonemason and to find work he'd been forced to travel to Newport. Her mother had just given birth to twin boys and had been slow to recover, so she had reluctantly taken to her bed, where according to Emily, she spent most of her time rocking the babies and weeping. Phoebe and Minnie had gained much pleasure from knowing that because of their hard work, the family would get through the winter with at least enough bread to sustain them and despite her mother's misgivings, Phoebe could think of no better charitable deed.

As she scrabbled around picking up the leftover bits of grain, Phoebe increasingly found her thoughts drifting to her mother, who would surely be sipping a cooling drink, whilst prattling on to anyone who would listen about how scandalised she felt at her daughter's unkempt appearance, whenever she returned home at the end of each day. She was thankful however, that even her mother had finally accepted that after weeks of such hard daily toil, her daughter should be allowed to attend the village festival, as long as Minnie's older brother promised to accompany them and Emily's mother would allow them to sleep in her home for the evening.

Phoebe's mother had always trusted Minnie's elder brother, the Reverend Jonathan Barwis. Much to his family's pride, he had just been confirmed in his new appointment at the much respected church of St Mary in Brading, allowing him to stay near his parents, whilst fulfilling his duties in the service of God. He was the only village boy that Phoebe's mother would ever trust with her daughter and when he had agreed to accompany them Phoebe had been delirious with excitement. For two long weeks, Jonathan Barwis had put aside his religious duties to help bring in the harvest, for the good of the parishioners. He insisted that he was doing the Lord's work, as helping to nourish their bodies with food from the land, was equally as important as nourishing their souls spiritually and the villagers loved him all the more for it. Early that morning, he had walked to the fields alongside his sister and her friends and had teased them about whether they could manage another day in the fields. Being strong and fit, he had been at the front with the other men throughout the day and the girls hadn't had the opportunity to talk to him for the rest of the day, though he would sometimes turn around and give them a smile, to ensure that they were well and still working hard.

Emily and Minnie only had eyes for the immature village boys, but Phoebe had her cap firmly set at Jonathan Barwis. He was only a couple of years older than her, yet he had always seemed wiser and more mature than his years, even when they were children, she had known that he was the only one for her. Unfortunately, Jonathan always given her the impression that he had only ever thought of her as the friend of his younger sister and nothing more, but she was determined to persevere, even if it took her years to turn his head. Phoebe was confident

11

that one day, he would realise that she was a child no longer and instead had grown into a young woman. She had spent many a restless night, dreaming of that day. Phoebe found Jonathan's quiet, studious air quite alluring, even though her friends preferred the louder and brasher village youths. He was a good listener; he always knew the right thing to do, helped anyone in their time of need and was more learned than the village dolts who thought only of taking their pleasure with a girl and where the next drink of ale was coming from. Most importantly to Phoebe, he looked handsome and distinguished, even when working in the fields. Every now and again, she would steal a look at him and marvel at the way golden hair shone brightly in the sunlight, peeking out from beneath his floppy cap and the broad shoulders, which made her feel weak at the knees whenever she was near him. Phoebe prided herself on successfully having kept her yearnings to herself. If Minnie and Emily were to find out how she felt, they would tease her mercilessly and worst still, Minnie would be sure to divulge her secret to her brother and Phoebe would never live down the shame, or be able to accept the rejection of her fragile heart, when she had been in love with him for so long.

A cheer went up from the rest of the crowd, momentarily taking Phoebe's mind off of Jonathan Barwis. "What's going on ?" She shouted to Emily, hardly daring to hope that it meant they were finished. "Look" Minnie, pulled her nearer, so that they could both see through a narrow gap in the sea of human bodies. Phoebe saw that the final sheaf was being loaded onto the cart and one of the old women of the village placed a perfect corn dolly on the very top, as was tradition. The cart in question had been decorated with flowers and colourful ribbons and it rumbled along to a chorus of cheers and clapping. The fields emptied, as everyone followed the cart and the smaller children danced and skipped, singing more joyously, now that they knew the hard work was over and the land had been good to them again, rewarding them for their efforts. Phoebe was certain that she would never be able to stand up straight ever again and her hands hurt unbearably from grasping at the wheat, yet she didn't regret a moment of it.

The farmer's wife Mary and their daughters Sarah and Lettice had been busy preparing the food, even before the sun itself had risen and their efforts adorned several trestle tables, placed just outside the open back door of their farmhouse.

Lanterns had been carefully hung like jewels amongst the tree branches and even though the daylight was only just beginning to fade, Phoebe thought that they made the setting look magical and hugged herself in delight at the scene. She had worn her favourite green dress with matching hat, around which she had fastened a shiny green ribbon and hoped that Jonathan Barwis would notice her at long last.

With the last sheaf safely stowed in the barn, the usually congenial Farmer Curtis was in an especially buoyant mood. He kept his speech short, mindful that they were all more than ready to fill their hungry bellies. He thanked them for their hard work and dedication, he finished by asking Jonathan to lead them in a prayer of thankfulness and welcomed them to enjoy his hospitality.

Even though, you were supposed to keep your eyes closed while you prayed, Phoebe rebelliously kept one eye open; to marvel with pride at how commanding and manly Jonathan was, when called upon to perform his religious duties.

Wine, beer, cider and gin flowed in copious amounts and after the succulent hams, several whole ducks, chickens, geese, slices of beef and haunches of pork had been consumed, along with the mountains of bread and honey pastries that melted on the tongue, the night began to cloak them in its darkness. The sky was cloudless and the stars shone in the inky blackness, showing the heavens in all their silvery glory.

As the shadows lengthened, the children, who were beginning to grow sleepy were carried home by their mothers and fathers, who themselves were feeling the effects of so much rich food and strong drink after working all day in the searing heat. Phoebe guessed that few of them would be up with the dawn, come the following morning and there would be more than a few sore heads in the village, though for the moment, their cheeks were ruddy and their faces plastered with smiles and not a shadow of regret among them. The lanterns shone brighter than the stars themselves, but even they couldn't compare to the gigantic orange and yellow harvest moon that hung low in the sky above them, almost close enough to touch. Once the families had retired, the young men and women of the village were free to carry on their merriment, without the risk of disapproving glances from the local parents.

Jonathan took his duties as chaperone seriously and he had remained by the girls' sides throughout the celebrations. Some of the young men had brought along their banjos and melodeons and the jaunty music carried on the warm air across the dark empty fields. As was customary, the farmer and his wife had been called upon to dance the first jig and as the evening wore on, the music slowed so that the couples could dance closer together, before they would discreetly disappear with stifled giggles into the darkness of the fields beyond, to make their own music in private.

Minnie and Emily had leapt at the chance to help Sarah and Lettice Curtis clear away the little that remained of the feast, whilst Phoebe had deliberately lingered over her own food, ensuring that they didn't get suspicious about why she seemed so desperate to remain by Jonathan's side. Phoebe privately suspected that they were secretly grateful to her for keeping Minnie's over-protective brother from following them into the farmhouse, where they loitered in the kitchen, giggling and fluttering their eyelashes at the farmer's two strapping sons, Alfred and Gabriel Curtis.

"The Lord has indeed blessed us with a good harvest this year, do you not think ?" She asked Jonathan, hoping that mentioning religious matters would help the conversation to flow. Since Minnie and Emily had disappeared inside to pursue the Curtis boys, Jonathan had seemed very ill at ease and Phoebe's spirits had fallen, as she realised that he probably wished he had been left alone with any one of the other village girls, rather than her. "The village will not go hungry through the winter" he muttered in confirmation, but she noticed that he had failed to acknowledge the Lord's hand in their good fortune, which for someone of his religious standing in the community seemed somewhat amiss. She was aware that he had imbibed much more than some of the other men and his eyes held a slight glassy quality. For some reason, he seemed more troubled than jovial and she wondered what she had done to put him into such a sombre mood. Phoebe had built up such expectations for the evening and none of them had included her beloved, to be sullen, morose and clearly uninterested and her heart sank in despair. Just as she was beginning to think that it might be best to go and find out what trouble Emily and Minnie were getting themselves into, he swayed in his seat, nearer towards her. "Would you like to take a walk with me ?" He whispered in her ear, making her shiver in surprised delight.

The noise from the music and the revellers, who clapped along, cheering loudly at the spectacle were all too busy to take any notice of them and she felt her heart leap with joy at the words she had longed for him to say. Phoebe nodded

15

in agreement, almost unable to believe he had actually noticed her at long last, it was the moment that she had dreamt of. She realised that his sullen mood was merely a result of his nervousness, borne of his feelings towards her and they would laugh about it one day, when they were living in wedded bliss.

For her part, Phoebe had started to feel the effects of the copious amount of wine she had consumed in her anxiety. It made her feel reckless and more than a little mischievous. She concentrated on preventing herself from swaying overly much, as she stood before him; ready for a romantic walk in the darkness. She was excited at the prospect of being completely alone with him for the first time ever, enfolded in the darkness where his sister and her friends wouldn't be able to find them. "Come on then" she said, trying to imitate a confidence that she didn't altogether feel and waited patiently, whilst he rose unsteadily to his feet.

The night wasn't as dark as it could have been, because of the huge harvest moon hanging low over the fields, outlining the shadows in a golden haze. As they slowly picked their way from the farmhouse, skirting the fields, they came upon an old barn falling apart from years of misuse and neglect. The blanket of stars could plainly be seen through the dilapidated roof, rendering it useless for storage or housing animals any longer. Despite the fact that she had her heart's desire holding onto her for support, Phoebe felt a slight sense of foreboding as Jonathan led her towards the barn entrance. She gulped in fear, as they entered the gloomy space and desperately tried to avoid peering into the darkest corners.

Jonathan had been silent throughout their walk and at first Phoebe had been concentrating on where she was stepping, rather than focusing on him, but once they had seated themselves down on an abandoned bale of straw,

Jonathan suddenly seemed more at ease, than he had all evening. "Is something wrong ?" She asked, sensing that whatever secrets he held, he might finally be ready to talk about them and then they might be able to concentrate on having fun together instead. "I am having a crisis of faith. I honestly do not know if the church is right for me and if that is the case, then I know not where I am destined. It is all I have ever known." He looked at her imploringly in the gloom, his eyes searching in desperation for the answer to his problems and she saw for the first time, just how tormented he was and the gap in their ages had never felt so wide to her before, she didn't even begin to know how to help him with his dilemma and hadn't bargained on such serious discussions, when they were finally alone. "But I thought you enjoyed being Reverend Barwis ? I thought it was all you had ever wanted to do ?" Phoebe was starting to think that their walk had been a bad idea after all. She was out of her depth, alone with a man who was wrestling with his inner demons, rather than wooing her. An image of her mother's disapproving face flew unbidden into her mind and Phoebe wondered what she would have to say, if she could see the exalted Jonathan Barwis, the trusted chaperone of her daughter, respected member of the clergy, in such a terrible state over his faith.

Sighing, he leant back, propping himself up on his elbows, whilst Phoebe looked nervously around at the imposing darkness and waited for him to speak. "I just agreed to what my mother and father demanded of me. I tried to be a good son, I could not disappoint them. My elder brother will be the one that inherits most of the estates and as I showed no aptitude for farming or managing livestock, they decided that I would be better placed in the church. I love my flock, but I feel like I am missing out on life. I just do not feel fulfilled of late. I do not know where my place should be. I no longer know where I could be truly happy." He swayed a little and looked around, as though he were expecting to find more ale, in the abandoned barn and seemed confused when he didn't. "How can you even question whether your place is in the church ?" Phoebe choked out. Her hands shook slightly, as her excitement mounted and her throat felt constricted by feelings of panic at his blasphemous speech. "For a start" he proclaimed loudly. "I spend all of my days thinking only of the love of God, it is all I know. I long to be loved in the physical sense, rather than merely the spiritual sense, just like other young men my age, just once. I have been watching you Phoebe, you were the prettiest girl at the feast, and I have always held you in the highest regard."

It was the most romantic thing that anyone had ever said to her and Phoebe was so thrilled, that she didn't even mind that he'd hiccupped a little at the end. Despite his fine words, his eyes seemed even more unfocused than they had before and she worried that he might collapse at any moment, robbing her of the opportunity to declare her love for him. The inside of the barn was so shadowy that it was difficult to make out just how intoxicated he was, but as he leant forward to kiss her, Phoebe closed her eyes and all of her fears, reason and judgement promptly deserted her.

She had dreamt of this moment for so long and she didn't want him to think that she was nought but a silly girl, too immature and unprepared to be loved as the woman she was. But in her fantasies, he hadn't been so drunk and they hadn't been hidden away in a rundown old barn that contained the lingering aroma of livestock and manure. She was aware that she really should prevent him from continuing, but her body tingled disloyally in response to his first advances and she was immediately lost.

Phoebe had always firmly believed that making love with the man she adored would leave her feeling enveloped in a

18

warming glow. That the act itself would bring them closer together and that afterwards, her beloved would hold her tightly in his arms and whisper softly that she was the only woman in the world for him, that they should be married without delay and he would declare himself to be totally under her spell.

The reality, she had found to her great dismay, was far different from her fanciful imaginings. Jonathan had been clumsy and she wondered if it had been his first time too, or whether the over consumption of ale had simply impaired his abilities. He had thrust himself inside of her several times in quick succession, grunted something unintelligible and then withdrew from her body abruptly, falling back against the wall of the barn and instead of whispered assurances and endearments, he had instantly begun to apologise and told her what a terrible mistake it had all been.

Phoebe lay in a state of shock, unable and unwilling to move. The lower half of her body thrummed with an unbearable burning sensation between her legs and a feeling of shame in the pit of her stomach. Jonathan insisted that they hurry back to the farmhouse before anyone realised they had disappeared and Phoebe was forced to follow at a run to catch up with him, as he marched off into the cool of the midnight air.

As they walked, he did not bother himself to enquire how she felt. Instead, he spent the time to pour out his own self-loathing and explained why the incident would be best kept a secret, in order to save both their reputations. He kept muttering that he would prostrate himself in church the next day and pray to the Lord for guidance, as though it were a mantra to save his mortal soul.

Phoebe listened to him and his words seemed to crawl over her like insects, covering her in feelings of wretchedness and disgust. She thought how disappointed her mother would feel and how enraged her father would surely be if they ever found out what had happened and decided that she would even go as far as to break off her friendship with Jonathan's sister Minnie and stay at home embroidering with her mother and be the dutiful daughter that her parents had always wished her to be. Phoebe felt cheated and used. She had allowed him to take her, believing that he was deeply in love with her and would use her honestly. It was supposed to be the beginning of their lives together, but he had lied and connived to get his own way, just as one of the village lads she despised, would have done. Phoebe shook her head in despair as she fought to understand how someone who was both so blessed and so virtuous, someone she had known all of her life, could turn out to be so manipulative. She struggled to give him the benefit of the doubt, for if she believed that he was remorseful over what had happened and had not planned to deceive her, she found that the pain and the shame of it were far easier to bear.

As they once again reached the safety of the farmhouse, the dancing was still in full swing with the musicians keeping up a lively tempo. The handful of villagers that remained, were now either too drunk to notice who was there with them, or else they had already split up into couples themselves and were too absorbed in each other and in making their own plans to sneak off, than to wonder where Phoebe and Jonathan had disappeared to. Not knowing what else to do, Phoebe absently followed Jonathan inside the farmhouse, where the warmth was a welcome change due to the dip in temperature outside. He had made her feel unworthy and soiled, but she had no option but to cleave to him until she was safely ensconced inside Emily's cottage.

Minnie and Emily were both softly snoring in front of the glowing fire, with two half-drunk tankards of ale next to

them on the large wooden table, the Curtis family were
nowhere to be seen and had obviously decided to retire to
their own beds and Phoebe felt like weeping at the
innocence she had lost, whilst her friends had slept.
Jonathan picked Minnie up with ease and carried her over
his right shoulder. Taking away Phoebe's virtue and the
walk back from the barn had helped him to recover his
sobriety and he was steady on his feet once more.

Phoebe gently roused Emily from her sleep and helped
her friend to stand. Though her senses had been dulled by
the drink and she was still half asleep, Emily allowed
Phoebe to lead her outside without argument. They waved
goodbye to the revellers and Minnie awoke fully when the
coolness of the outside air reached her, after the cosiness
and warmth of Farmer Curtis' hearth and she batted her
brother's back, demanding that he put her down and let her
walk by herself.

Whilst Phoebe and Jonathan had been missing from the
party, Minnie and Emily had taken full advantage of their
freedom by busily flirting with the strapping Curtis twins
and they whispered and giggled to one another
conspiratorially, sneaking glances backwards at Phoebe
and Jonathan, to ensure they couldn't overhear their
secrets. Phoebe had never had an argument with Minnie or
Emily in the whole of their friendship, but for the first time
she felt a burning hatred, as she watched them.

Apart from the physical discomfort, she felt isolated from
her silly sniggering friends and despite their excitement,
Phoebe had no doubt that they were still chaste and it made
her want to rush home and scrub herself clean. They should
have looked after her, but instead they'd been too absorbed
in their own assignations to save her. She decided that she
would attend church as soon as she could and pray to the
Lord for his divine forgiveness, plead with him that no one
else would ever uncover her secret shame; 'at least' she

thought to herself mournfully, 'I can rely on Jonathan Barwis not to go around the village bragging of his conquest.'

*　　*　　*

Weeks later, Phoebe awoke in the early hours of the still morning, with a start. The same dream had been troubling her sleep, every night since the harvest. It always began in exactly the same way, with Jonathan Barwis being her friend, before he would suddenly transform into a creeping devil, complete with wings. The monster would steal her soul away with a sickening smile upon his face. During the daytime, Phoebe had the ability to push away such dark thoughts, but at night they crawled in when she was powerless to stop them. Phoebe had spent the past few weeks permanently at her mother's side and convinced herself that she could be happy, as long as she stayed within the protected confines of her own home. She hadn't wanted to put Minnie in the impossible situation of having to choose between her best friend and her brother, so she made the agonising decision for her and had resolutely shunned any of Minnie's invitations. Happily, her mother had passed no comment on her sudden reclusive habits and ensured that she was kept busy with sewing and reading and the suitable pastimes she had always tried to impress upon her daughter.

The nightmare had awoken her as usual, but for the first time she felt queasy and was forced to grit her teeth firmly together to prevent herself from vomiting. Her breasts were swollen and tender, but they often felt sore when she was due to start her flux, so she wasn't unduly worried. Over the next few weeks she waited with mounting anxiety, but her women's courses did not come and her symptoms grew steadily worse. Gritting her teeth no longer worked as prevention and she was physically sick on most mornings. She found that she could no longer face the aroma of hot tea and most foods that she actually craved, tasted unappetisingly like metal in her mouth, except for honey slathered onto freshly baked bread, which she ate in copious amounts. For weeks she had cloaked herself in denial, but she could no longer hide from the fact that she was pregnant with Jonathan Barwis' child.

Phoebe spent endless hours kneeling on the freezing church floor in front of the candlelit altar, praying for help and guidance. But no response came from the silent high arches on every side of the nave and only the implacable pale, Isle of Wight stone stared silently back at her. She had been in love with Jonathan, dreamt of a future with him and he had taken advantage of her feelings and used her in the worst way possible. She saw now, that he had hidden his evil nature beneath a religious man's costume and she despaired of what would happen when her parents found out that she was carrying an illegitimate child.

Knowing that she couldn't keep it to herself any longer, she stood in the doorway watching her mother sitting alone writing a letter to one of her aunts. Phoebe's heart hammered in her chest and she silently prayed for the ground to open up and swallow her. When she looked up and saw Phoebe's wretched expression, she abandoned her correspondence, watching her daughter intently. "Come and sit down my dear, you look positively unwell. Where on earth have you been for all this time ? Were you with Minnie and Emily ? You haven't seen them for a while, has there been a disagreement ?" Phoebe's hands shook unbearably and the room span as she fought against the black void of unconsciousness that threatened to engulf her. "No" she whispered, slumping into a seat and shaking her head at the drink her mother held out to her. Phoebe had always been in no doubt that her mother was a harsh woman, but her father was far more austere and likely to react with violence, so in order to break the news she decided that it would be better to appeal to her mother's slightly softer nature, in the first instance. She desperately hoped that even though her mother would be understandably upset and disappointed at first, she would eventually prove to be an ally. Phoebe had spent her sleepless nights finding a path through the terrible future that awaited her. She had decided to raise the baby at home and keep the outside world from discovering her shame. After a few months, they could convince their friends and neighbours that the child belonged to a cousin from Freshwater who had died, leaving it motherless and the Downer's had selflessly offered to take the child in and raise it as their own. "Please my dear" said her mother, stroking her cheek. "I know something is wrong. It cannot be so bad that you cannot tell me about it, surely."

Phoebe had been carrying around the weight of her guilty secret for weeks and she was mentally and physically exhausted. "M...m...mother" she stuttered, taking a deep breath. "I'm going to have a baby and I am so sorry. I've been so scared." Her words resounded like a thunderclap in the room. "But how could this happen ?" Her mother's voice which had sounded caring and compassionate only minutes before, was now unnaturally shrill. "It cannot be possible. You must be mistaken." She shook her head dismissively as though the matter was at an end. "I'm not mistaken. I'm so sorry. Please forgive me." Her mother continued in her state of denial, determined not to listen. "If you were with child, there would have to be a boy involved and you have no time for the village boys. You spend all your time running around with Minnie and that Emily girl from Bembridge."
"It happened at the harvest celebration. I went for a walk and a stranger attacked me. I believe he came from another

village to help, no one else seemed to recognise him. I was too ashamed to tell anyone and I thought that I would eventually be able to put it behind me and no one need ever know what had happened." Before her mother could reply, her father stormed angrily into the room, his complexion was a beetroot colour and Phoebe worried that he would have an apoplexy. "Tell me that I am mistaken in what I just heard you say," he bellowed as he strode to stand in front of her, staring at his daughter's bowed head. "Tell me! Do you or do you not carry a bastard in your belly ?"

His coarse language made her mother stir uneasily in her seat, but even in the depths of her fear, Phoebe noted that she failed to speak up on her daughter's behalf. "Well ?" He roared and Phoebe knew that the longer she stayed silent, the angrier he would become, he had clearly heard most of their conversation anyway. "It is true" she muttered. "I was savagely attacked by a stranger at the bringing in of the harvest." Tears began to run down her face and she wiped them absentmindedly aside, summoning up the courage to look directly at her father. His cheeks were ruddy with temper and his black hair which had just begun to turn grey at the temples, looked messy and unkempt, as he vented his fury. "I want you out!" He barked at her. "I will not have you living under my roof. You are a disgrace to this family. We have worked hard to elevate our family in society. I will not have a stupid girl tearing all of that down by making us the centre of the town's scandal." Phoebe looked around in distress, but her mother simply sat as rigid as a statue, watching the proceedings but having no part in them. "Where would I go ?" She implored, her dreams of raising her child in the family home, now completely evaporated. "As you are my daughter and you claim that you were attacked and not wanton, I will give you one of our cottages. You may go and live in it and make a fresh start.

25

You should think yourself lucky that I shall also give you a generous amount of money to take with you. However, once that runs out I don't want to see you here again. We want nothing to do with you and I must demand that you never mention your association with this family, to anyone. Ever."

Her tears had ceased falling and her fear had given way to anger and indignation. Phoebe hurriedly packed her clothes, anxious to be away, but not thinking about what her future held. As a last thought, she grabbed her sewing kit, after all, her clothes wouldn't fit her petite frame for very much longer and she would need to make some adjustments to accommodate her increasing girth. As she flew towards the door, she saw that her father had left a large purse filled with money for her. Uncharacteristically, her mother appeared and kissed her perfunctorily on the cheek. Phoebe thought for one moment that her mother was about to embrace her for the first time in her life, but instead she simply said "there is a cart waiting for you outside. I wish you luck" and without another word, she turned and walked away, without even a backward glance.

Phoebe cried all the way through the jolting journey to the front door of her Bembridge cottage. Her father had been generous, despite his anger. Her new home was beautiful and so spacious that it could have accommodated two whole families. It was a sturdy structure, with a thick golden thatched roof on top and had she seen it under any other circumstances, she thought that she would have fallen in love with it at first sight, but her woes were too big to allow room for any other emotion.

Gradually as the days passed and she cleaned and scrubbed the cottage, it began to feel like home and although she missed her parents terribly, she began to feel excited and grateful for the child that was slowly growing in her stomach and having the freedom to live her life on her own terms at last.

Chapter 1
Bembridge, Isle of Wight, August 16th 1827

The mellow sun peeked through the dense emerald canopy of the leafy trees overhead, dappling the parched earth with light and making me narrow my eyes against the yellowy white harshness. Spring had arrived at long last and I felt as restless and eager as the bright green daffodil shoots that were just beginning to eagerly push their way up through the stirring ground beneath me, in the first bursts of warm weather across the island after the cold, hard days of winter.

Just ahead of me on that path, I heard the familiar sounds of women talking animatedly and children giggling mischievously, just out of sight. Slowing my stride a little, I hung back, so I could enjoy some peace for just a little while longer. Everyone in Bembridge except for my beloved mother, had turned out for the most exciting event ever to happen in our little village in living memory and the locals were forever stopping me, enquiring after my poor mother's health and telling me of their ailments, so I hoped to hold them off for as long as possible. The weather was expected to remain fine and I certainly didn't intend to waste a minute of this exciting day.

Sundays were always my favourite day of the week, but my fellow villagers resented making the arduous four mile journey over to Brading to get to St Mary's Church. There was a horse boat that ferried people across the marshes from one side to the other, but it only operated at low tide and on fine days, so it wasn't the most reliable mode of transport. In the long dark winter months, the journey was totally impossible and our sleepy little village would find itself completely isolated from the rest of our beloved island for months on end and we became a little island all of our own. I had always loved the little church of St Mary and found a great deal of comfort within its hallowed walls, but not many felt the same way. In the past few years the population of the village had exploded, due to so many wealthy people deciding to settle in the area and the need had arisen for our own place of worship right here in Bembridge. After a determined effort to raise funds, the new chapel of ease had finally been completed and it really hasn't sunk in for any of us yet, that we no longer have to carry out such an onerous journey any longer. Most of the money had been donated by the extremely wealthy Edward Wise, who'd donated the substantial sum of thirteen thousand pounds for the cause and had even given us the land for the church to be built upon, his wife Amelia therefore had the honour of laying the foundation stone for the chapel last year. Edward has just inherited his uncle's large estate and is using his new found wealth to improve the lives of the people of Bembridge, I even heard a rumour last week, that he is intending to build a school now that the chapel is finished. Edward has also rented out two and a half acres of his land for the sum of five pounds a year and stated that this money would be put towards the stipend for the new curate of the chapel. His generosity didn't stop there however, he also managed to persuade his good friend Charles Grant to donate the sum of one hundred pounds for the cause, and another friend of theirs named Admiral Hammond provided the stone to make the building itself. Then, the Admiral's friend Charles Dennett, transported the heavy stones from the ledge over to the site of the chapel at no charge. Our community had always been close and strived to come together for a common purpose, but there was definitely a benefit to having new wealthy villagers eager to be accepted and willing to provide us with their services, in order to stop us being so suspicious of the newcomers.

My father had confided in me a few days ago, that the Trinity Board were having a meeting to discuss whether they would provide a thousand pounds specifically for the building of a spire, for the ships of the Royal Navy to use as a seamark by which they could safely navigate the islands treacherous waters, though it was hard to imagine how the building could look even more impressive than it already did. Even the well-known architect Jonathan Nash, had given his plans for the new building for free, to our lowly village and was used by an architect from Portsmouth called Jacob Owen for the building of the new chapel of ease. All of this attention from such noted men, sent our sense of pride soaring, for this little forgotten corner of the Isle of Wight. Jonathan Nash had built his own island home, naming it East Cowes Castle and I had heard talk amongst the villagers of how fine it was with its lofty towers and enviable views across the Solent. There had been much excitement amongst the village elders that they had managed to secure Nash's expertise. He was the favourite architect of none other than King George the Fourth himself, the man responsible for developing and designing the most lavish and important new buildings in London. Nash had improved the Royal Pavilion in Brighton and was currently in the middle of working on Buckingham Palace itself. For him to give his valuable time for free was a real coup for the village and there had been celebrations aplenty at the Olde Village Inne, ever since the good news had been announced. I had even heard that there had been fighting amongst some of our Bembridge boys and a group of drunken Sandown lads who thought our village had got a bit above themselves.

Men had laboured on the building for months, hauling the limestone from the Bembridge ledge. After so much effort, todays celebrations were the culmination of all the hard work and expense. The church was to be consecrated by none other than George Pretyman Tomline, the Bishop of Winchester himself and we were determined to enjoy seeing our sleepy little Bembridge honoured with the services of two of the greatest men in the country.

As I rounded the corner, I saw everyone I knew assembled in front of the new building, underneath a sea of hats and ribbons. The crowd were dressed in their finest clothes and the children danced around, as though it were a feast day. The holiday atmosphere brought a smile to my face, yet I couldn't help but feel a slight pang of remorse that my mother had been far too ill to accompany me to see such splendour and excitement. I tried hard to commit every detail to memory, so that I would be able to recreate the whole spectacle, when I finally returned home.

The limestone of the chapel shimmered in the sun as the stone structure rose out of the ground, making it the most impressive building ever to have been built in Bembridge, though I found it impossible to imagine a finer church anywhere else in the whole world. A low wall has been built around the chapel, with room inside the grounds for the graves which would be laid there for eternal rest. I shuddered at the thought as I look around at the assembled throng and wondered who will be the first of them to be laid inside the chapel confines. The stained glass in the elegant windows is illuminated by the suns rays, as though God himself were smiling on our endeavours. Beyond the sturdy elms, and behind the open gates, I could just make out Edward Wise standing outside the chapel with his wife Amelia by his side proudly smiling and their three young sons looking uncomfortable in their finery who kept tugging relentlessly at the their collars, despite the angry glances their mother kept shooting in their direction and I had no doubt that beneath her cheerful façade, she was planning to have words with them in the privacy of their own home later. A few steps from them were a group of well dressed, serious looking men in long double breasted coats and tall hats standing together, I didn't recognise them so I guessed they were probably members of the Trinity Board, come to inspect their latest potential investment. Next I spotted Jonathan Nash, his greying hair was receding, but his deep brown eyes twinkled with good humour, making him look much younger than his years and he seemed genuinely pleased to be given so much praise for his newest creation. I watched him accepting the gratitude of the villagers who thanked him for taking the time to join us on our special day, when the king would surely be needing him too. Beside Nash, was a man known far less well to us Bembridge inhabitants, it was the Bishop of Winchester. The Bishop was a tall broad man, with a full head of thick white hair, which I privately thought, made it seem as though a huge cloud permanently hovered around his head. He possessed a brooding countenance and a thin hooked nose set above small dark eyes, however he looked resplendent in his vestments and the great and good of Bembridge were fawning over him as if he were an anointed king. I watched him briefly, as he scrutinised the new building, deftly avoiding the villagers who had turned out for the occasion. I wanted to believe that he seemed aloof because he had pressing holy matters on his mind, whilst the thing uppermost in the villager's minds was the hog roast outside the Olde Village Inne, later in the morning, I didn't want to think uncharitably about him, when he was such an important holy man. The Bishop had once been a close friend and adviser to William Pitt the Younger and my chest swelled with pride as I saw my father standing next to two men who were held in such high esteem by the king himself. Bembridge was indeed honoured to have such auspicious guests and I was grateful to be a part of it.

My father, Jonathan Barwis, had been moved from his place at Niton to preside over the new church and my heart leapt in delight at having my father so close. I hoped that we would be able to build an even closer relationship now that I could visit him at the new church whenever I desired. I'm extremely proud of my father, despite the shame that being the illegitimate daughter of Reverend Jonathan Barwis has undoubtedly brought upon me. Being near my father wasn't the only cause for my excitement though, my mother permitted me to wear my latest gown and I fervently hoped that it would help me to catch the eye of William Gould. In my humble opinion William is the most handsome young man in the village and the consecration of the new church was the perfect time to seek him out. My new dress was a vivid scarlet, with dark blue edging and long pale blue under sleeves covering my arms, I looked a perfect picture of gay abandon and modesty combined. Atop my long golden hair, I wore a scarlet hat surrounded by a navy blue ribbon, perfectly matching my new gown and my feet were comfortably clad in navy silk shoes, bound to a wooden heel, of which I was most proud.

My mother, never discussed her side of the family and all I'd managed to discover, was that they were wealthy and when she had told them she was to be an unwedded mother, they had wanted no more to do with her and cast her out of the home. I knew that they had given her some money and the home I had grown up in, whilst my grandparents had moved to the village of Carisbrooke. The small village overlooked by the great castle was far enough away from their errant daughter and illegitimate granddaughter to feel respectable again, as a result I have spent all of my life, knowing that although I am loved, I am also my family's darkest secret and their deepest shame. I watched my mother struggle to keep us clothed and fed throughout the years and had always felt a deep sense of guilt at the sacrifices she'd made for me. My mother had always done her very best to manage the money and to earn us a livelihood and although we had never considered ourselves to be wealthy, I knew that we fared far better than most families in the village, largely because my mother has always been careful not to arouse jealousy or suspicion in others. Business has thankfully always been brisk, but I'm fairly certain that my mother often earns extra money by means that she likes to keep from me, but despite her secrecy, I have my suspicions that it involves the darker side of magic and communing with those who have already passed over.

Despite our close bond, it has always a source of tension between my mother and I that I love to visit my father. Although she would never go so far as to actually prevent me from being close to him, I knew that my mother was jealous of our close father-daughter relationship. Despite the hurt it causes, I can't help but love the dignified, quiet man who wears his shame like a heavy cloak. My parents had never explained to me what had really happened between them or why they had never married and so I'd been left with no choice but to give them both the benefit of the doubt and loved them equally. My eyes clouded with pain, as I thought of my mother, lying in her four poster bed coughing unrelentingly, trying to read the psalms of David, waiting for my return. Whenever she is ill, I am wholly responsible for keeping the cottage spotless, cooking the meals, maintaining our little vegetable and herb patch, protecting the livestock, dealing with the endless demands of customers, the constant replenishment of stock and caring for my mother. I would often come home to find one of the villagers beside her bed with the heavy green drapes tied back, wanting their runes read or asking advice on one problem or another. People only came to us, when they were ill or in desperate need, it made for a rewarding life for my mother, but a burden to myself when I was frequently called on to cope alone. As an adult, my mother had never enjoyed good health, but even by her standards, she seemed to be increasingly suffering with one malady after another of late. It's a dreadful irony that no matter how adept my mother is at healing others, she seems incapable of curing herself. She is losing her tenuous grasp on this life and it can surely only be a matter of time before myself and the good villagers of Bembridge lose her forever. Shaking away my morbid thoughts on such a beautiful day, I decided that I would pick her some flowers on my way home. My mother always says that there is nothing so sad in this life, which the sight of a daffodil couldn't cheer. Privately, I don't think she would have accompanied me even if she weren't confined to her bed. She had taken the news that my father was to be the first incumbent of the new chapel and would therefore be a familiar daily sight in Bembridge, particularly badly. My mother had instantly taken to her bed when a gossiping villager had divulged the news and not risen since. She is intent on lying behind the thick curtains of her bed feeling sorry for herself and so I was forced to come alone.

Squeezing my way through the tightly packed throng, towards the front of the crowd, where the most prestigious members of our village were standing beside the visitors, to bless the new building. I searched the faces, but couldn't see William anywhere. The people nearest to the church were the local business owners and the wealthiest Bembridge families such as the Knowles and the Dennetts, so I pushed back through the crowd until I reached a space where the mass of villagers had begun to thin out slightly. Searching the faces, I saw a gaggle of excited girls standing in a group around a tall, young man with broad shoulders, smiling easily down at them. Each of the girls had their backs turned towards me, but even from this distance, I recognised Elizabeth, Sally, Alice and noisiest of them all, Harriet Morey.

There had once been a time when I thought that Harriet and I might be actually friends, but I found out very quickly that I was sadly mistaken. It was as if it had only happened yesterday, it's so clearly etched in my memory. We had both been around ten years old at that first meeting, all those years ago. Harriet had just been sent to live with her grandparents, her mother had found it hard to cope with so many children and Harriet who had always been somewhat of a challenge, had been given over into her grandparent's care, in the hope that she might settle down. Several years later, her parents and siblings also came to live with them, when they eventually lost their home in Newport. My mother had told me to be on the lookout for the new girl in the village and make her feel welcome, just in case she was feeling scared by all the strangers in the village and miserable at having to leave her parents and siblings behind. Her words had made a deep impression on me. I knew how it felt, not to have two parents around and to feel like an outsider in your own village. My heart immediately went out to the Morey's granddaughter. I've always tried to help others in need, like the good Christian girl my parents raised me to be, so I hurriedly set out to make a new friend. Taking a bowl of strawberries with me, I made my way to Harriet's grandparent's home, humming as I went, trying to see the village through a newcomer's eyes. Washing blew in the breeze, making the clothes dance eerily as if they had a life of their own, the older women sat outside their homes gossiping with neighbours, whilst children played games like hide and seek. A stonemason walked past, carrying his hammer and chisel in his bag and as he nodded to me in greeting I wondered how anyone could bear to live anywhere other than Bembridge. Surely there was no greater place in the whole world than my own friendly little village, when the birds were singing and the sun was shining. As I neared the cottage, I saw a fat ginger cat with white patches sitting on the window ledge, lazily licking its front paw in a warm pool of sunshine. Looking up from the cat, I spotted an unfamiliar girl standing just outside of the door. I had just found Harriet Morey.

Near to Harriet, I spied Jack and Tom, two brothers whose parents ran the old Olde Village Inne and I could see from the look on their faces that they were up to their usual mischief. I eyed them warily and prayed that they wouldn't be tempted to cause trouble for the poor new girl. I was in a hurry to make Harriet's acquaintance, so I ignored the two young boys and focused resolutely on making friends with someone who must surely be feeling wretched and lonely. Harriet's face was obscured by her shoulder length, thinning brown hair, as she turned in my direction, I opened my mouth to say hello, but instead, I heard Tom yell out. "There she is, the prettiest girl in the village. How about a kiss for a young boy in love ?" Harriet completely ignored me, even though by this time, I was standing right in front of her and her head shot back around with a wicked gleam in her slanted green eyes, which I noticed were set far too wide apart, above her short snub nose. Harriet looked directly at Jack and Tom and bestowed her brightest smile on them. Far from seeming to be a girl feeling unwelcome, she sauntered closer to where the two boys sat watching her with mounting amusement. "So which one of you might be in love with me then?" She asked loudly, full of confidence in her own charms. "Or perhaps it is both of you that want to claim a kiss ? Come on then, who's first ?" The boys slid off of the wall, clutching their stomachs, laughing wildly. I watched in horror, as Harriet's demeanour collapsed, when Tom pointed at her, completely incredulous. "Why on earth would you ever think that we would be talking to you ?" "As if" chimed in Jack. "We were talking to her." Harriet followed the direction of Jack's grubby little finger and finally noticed me standing uncomfortably, pity etched all over my face. Harriet's eyes were burning with pure hatred, as she faced me, the cause of her embarrassment. I blushed furiously, desperately wishing I were anywhere else, I wanted to run away, but found that my feet had been firmly rooted to the spot, I couldn't have moved, even if my life had depended on it. Harriet stormed off into her grandparent's home, with the sound of the boys' laughter still ringing loudly in her ears and her cheeks flaming with mortification. For my part, I was left standing alone with the strawberries still in my hands. From that moment on, Harriet had never let me forget just how much she despised me. I felt dreadful, but my pity seemed to incense her all the more and it seemed that there was nothing I could ever do to make amends.

The next time we met, had been two weeks later and that had given Harriet Morey more than enough time to find out the village gossip. I had been on my way to church in Brading, when I was stopped in my tracks, by Harriet and her cronies blocking my path. Instantly I felt my senses tingle at the prospect of imminent danger. My instinct was to turn around and run as far as possible in the other direction, but in the end pride won out and I stood my ground, hoping that they wouldn't notice my hands shaking uncontrollably. "Morning" I said, fighting to control the level of my voice and trying not give myself away. I looked at the group expectantly, waiting for them to make the next move. "I've just been hearing" said Harriet, her voice louder and more shrill than usual, while her new friends, Elizabeth and Sally grinned at one another, both thoroughly enjoying the spectacle. "That your mother seduced a certain unsuspecting Reverend Barwis and got herself pregnant. She thought she could trick him into marriage, but found out that she had been sorely mistaken. When she begged him to marry her, he decided he couldn't face a lifetime of being shackled to such a shrew and hurriedly married someone else instead, so your mother's family cast her out in shame and she was forced to bring her bastard up in Bembridge, all alone. Now I know I'm new here, but tell me, have I got all my details correct?"

Being taunted over my illegitimacy was nothing new to me. I had dealt with it for all of my life, but the abuse had never centred in on my mother before and the lies were too much for me to bear. Especially when my poor gentle mother was struck down with a terrible illness, unable to sit up in her bed by herself, let alone defend her reputation. Without thinking I had flown at Harriet, ready to slap her hard across the face, but Sally and Elizabeth had stepped in between us and prevented me from carrying out my attack. The look on Harriet's face had been one of pure smugness and my total humiliation had been complete. A crowd had gathered out nowhere and I had felt my cheeks burning with shame and tears welling in my eyes, stopping me from seeing properly. "That isn't true, it's a gross lie. How dare you?" Harriet planted her hands on her hips and assumed the air of someone explaining something difficult to a particularly dim child. "Did your mother sleep with Reverend Barwis, when she was not married or even betrothed to him?" She tapped her foot as she waited for my reply, causing several of the onlookers to chuckle loudly at her audacity. Every pair of eyes turned toward me in unison. "Yes" I whispered, but Harriet wasn't going to let me off so lightly. "I'm sorry Molly, I didn't quite catch that, could you speak up please. Did your mother sleep with Reverend Barwis, even though they were not married ?" My eyes burning with anger, I faced my enemy and vowed to make Harriet pay for her insults, one way or another. "Yes" I answered defiantly, through gritted teeth, jutting my chin out in temper. The crowd were thoroughly enjoying the unexpected display and Harriet held them all in her thrall. "Did your father marry your mother or did he in fact marry someone else ?"

"He is married to another woman." I spat back, wanting to scratch Harriet's eyes out. "Then you cannot say that I have lied, can you ?" At a nod from Harriet, Sally and Elizabeth stepped back and allowed me to push my way through the crowd. I fled home, crying tears of rage, feeling as though the whole world had colluded with Harriet Morey against me and my beloved mother. Over the following years, there had been a handful of similar incidents between the two of us. Harriet usually came off the worst in an encounter, which only increased her spite, tenfold with every lost battle.

Watching the girls now in the joyous crowd, before the new church building, I felt the same warning flashes run up and down my spine. Elizabeth moved nearer to whisper something into Sally's ear and my eyes met those of the handsome boy the girls had surrounded; it was William Gould. He worked in his family's shipbuilding business and had been the object of my desire for several months, ever since I had first noticed him strolling through the village. I stared a little longer than was proper for a young lady and blushed a deep scarlet, which I knew perfectly matched the shade of my dress, under the curious scrutiny of his vivid hazel eyes. Looking away coyly, my gaze fell upon the angered face of Harriet Morey. Her countenance was a mask of icy hatred in complete contrast with William's warm welcoming expression. His heavy dark brown curls framed his square chinned jaw and I thought that trying to look at him, was as difficult a task as looking directly into the face of the sun. Whenever I looked in his direction and saw the beauty of his features, I often forgot to breathe. His sparkling eyes had immediately changed from boredom to frank interest and in that instant, he was totally transformed by his radiant smile. I completely forgot the rest of the village and my world reduced down to just William and myself. The atmosphere turned decidedly frosty and the girls reminded me of geese when they were particularly angry and defensive, before they viciously chased their enemies and attacked them. Harriet spun towards me with Elizabeth, Sally and Alice as always, directly behind her. From the way they turned, I could tell that the girls were seemingly intent on shooing me away, as if I were an eagle about to swoop in and steal their prey. Bracing myself against the inevitable onslaught, I felt someone beside me, gently tugging at my arm. Surprised, I turned with relief, to find my best friend, Hannah standing beside me with a furious look upon her face. Hannah's dark brown eyes glared at Harriet, in open opposition, leaving everyone in no doubt that she was more than a match for any of them. I watched as a brief flicker of uncertainty passed over Harriet's unbecoming features. "Come along Mol" Hannah said brightly, though her gaze was still firmly fixed on the now silent group of girls, daring them to open their mouths in her presence. "The doors are open, we should go in now to ensure that we have a good seat." I smiled with gratitude and allowed Hannah to lead me into the cool confines of the new village chapel. I was not about to fight like a common fishwife today of all days and definitely not whilst William Gould was watching me. It might make him think that I was not marrying material and I didn't want anything to jeopardise his opinion of me. It was hard enough, when I carried the stigma of illegitimacy around with me all of the time, I couldn't afford to rock the boat, at least until I had caught him. Arm in arm, we disappeared in through the gates amongst the throng of excited villagers.

I looked around and admired the cool confines of the chapel. I loved the solid comfort of the stonework, the tang of the salt air that blew in from Brading Haven, but I would have adored the building no matter what, because it was an enduring link with my father. Although the building itself was new, it already held the familiar aroma of the incense, the sun streamed through the narrow colourful windows and the welcoming sense of God's presence were a balm to my soul, filling me with wellbeing and spiritual warmth. Taking a seat next to Hannah, I looked up and saw my father standing just behind the altar. His head was bathed in a beam of coloured light, cast by one of the windows and to my biased view he looked like an angel, with his glimmering halo evident for all to see, proclaiming his brilliance and high standing in the eyes of the Lord, or at least that was my opinion of him. As he met my gaze, my father smiled and my heart leapt with happiness, when I saw how his eyes crinkled at the edges, the way they always did whenever he looked at me. I knew my father seldom smiled and I was proud that I could raise his spirits. All too swiftly, my happiness diminished as I noticed a look of shame pass over his hollow features. I knew without a shadow of a doubt that my father was proud of me and that he loved me very much, but I was also equally sure that I was also the source of his constant humiliation and a walking reminder to him and everyone else of his greatest sin.

*   *   *

Looking at his daughter across the nave, Reverend Barwis of Niton felt a leap of gladness in his heart, swiftly followed by a wave of shame that threatened to engulf him in its ferocity. This child, who clearly resembled him, was the undeniable proof that he had once indulged in a moment of temporary weakness, during a crisis of faith and had succumbed to earthly temptations and feminine wiles. He told himself that he had only transgressed because he had been a young man, needing to experience such depths of depravity so that he could find his way back into the light of God's love and use his experience to help other troubled souls. The morning after the night of disgrace, his head had pounded abominably and he cursed the day that he had ever met Phoebe Downer and her wanton behaviour. Seeking absolution, he had wholeheartedly repented, begging God for forgiveness, until his knees had finally given out on the cold stone of the church floor. It had all been for naught, it was one lesson that the Lord hadn't been willing to let him forget. Ten months later, just when he believed that he might be left to live a peaceful life in God's service, Phoebe Downer had come looking for him. She had waited beneath the old lychgate outside of his church, which at the time had been the church of St Jonathan the Baptist, in the pretty little village of Niton, where he had fled to escape his tortured memories. Phoebe had stepped out in front of him, changing his life forever. Without any small talk or preamble, she announced that he was the father of her four week old baby girl. His legs gave way in shock and he found himself once more on his knees, praying to God for guidance and mercy. He was still assuaged by guilt for what had happened and he was well aware that Phoebe felt nothing but revulsion for him after he had confessed that he had already married his wife Jane Allanby. A good woman from a wealthy family, a match that his parents had chosen for him. He had silently watched Phoebe leave, her shoulders lowered and her spirit crushed, she had been left with no choice but to bring their

43

child up alone and he was in no position to help her. His newly wedded wife would hardly be pleased if he started giving away their money to another woman and his lovechild, especially when she was having such trouble conceiving herself. He had no idea how he would explain the news to her and he feared how the new Mrs Barwis would cope with even a hint of any scandal. Through his family he heard that Phoebe had been shunned by the villagers when she had first moved into the village of Bembridge and he offered her what little financial help he could afford to send without his wife discovering his secret. Finally he had been forced into confessing to her about the secret child he had fathered and the news had not been accepted well. God had indeed worked in mysterious ways, as he found himself ordered to fill a position in the very same village as his daughter and her mother. Jane was unhappy enough that he was to be working in Bembridge of all places, but she had flatly refused to live in the same village as Phoebe and Molly and so he was forced to travel to and from his new home in Brading each day, with the inconvenience of staying at the inn when the route was totally impassable. He had been happy to do so, to spare his wife the indignity of having her nose rubbed in his misdeeds on a daily basis and they had reached a fragile peace on the matter. Despite the shock of the news and the marital discord that had happened as a consequence, he had been unexpectedly filled with wonder at the God given miracle that was his daughter, but it was a double edged sword that threatened to drown him in a pool of remorse, every time he looked at her.

*   *   *

Sitting in the church, I found myself completely mesmerised by my father's sermon. I loved the way his melodic voice bounced off of the walls and the high vaulted ceilings and I loved hearing his voice soar, as he led them in song. It was when I watched him standing in front of his congregation that I felt the most proud of him. My father's wife was barren and the knowledge of her own failings made her even more spiteful where I was concerned and so meetings with him were fewer and far between than ever, as Jane spiralled ever downwards into paranoia and hatred.

Even though it had never been publicly acknowledged, the villagers knew that he was my father, yet they seemed happy to condemn my mother rather than a man of the church. My father had been readily accepted by the villagers, after all, in the eighteen years that we had been living amongst them, there had been other village scandals which had diminished my parent's own and it no longer seemed so horrifying to most of them, that he had fathered me out of wedlock. Everyone was perfectly happy to lay the blame solely at my mother's door for enticing him, getting herself pregnant and generally bringing about her own downfall. As they saw it, he was simply a man, with a man's weaknesses, how could he possibly be to blame. She was a woman who had happily lain down with an older man who hadn't professed love for her, let alone proposed marriage to her and allowed him to have his way with her. Whilst the older generation sought to blame her for being an unwed mother, the younger generation it seemed, were even more eager to hold me accountable, for being born out of wedlock.

The service finished all too soon and Hannah nudged me painfully in the ribs, making me jump, as I stared at my father in awe. "Come on, I don't plan on spending all the day in here, when my stomach is rumbling like thunder." I laughed and shook my head. Hannah was perpetually thinking about food, her mother complained that she ate more than her brothers after a hard days labour in the field. We made our way through the crowd to the main door, which now stood wide open, beckoning us to venture back outside, into the spring morning.

Shielding my eyes as I walked into the brilliant sunshine, I found myself temporarily blinded and bumped straight into someone standing slightly to the left of me. Turning to apologise, I once again found myself looking straight into the eyes of William Gould. I stared, completely nonplussed as he pushed a stray curl out of his eyes, watching me with amusement. His eyes were the exact same colour as ale when the sun shines directly through it and the way his smile completely disarmed me, made all reason fly right out of my head. "I enjoyed listening to your pa" he said, almost shyly. I hadn't even realised that Hannah had released her hold on my arm and taken a step or two backwards into the shadows of the church walls, giving us some privacy to talk alone. The rest of the village filed out of the church, passing by without comment as they made their way down towards the Olde Village Inne for the hog roast and celebrations. "I did too, but then I'm very proud of him," I muttered quietly, aware that most of the congregation would condemn me for publicly acknowledging my father. It was one thing for my paternity to be common knowledge in gossiping circles, but quite another for it to be spoken aloud in polite company. "How is your ma ? I've heard she's been unwell." William rushed on, suddenly aware of the awkwardness that talking about my father would bring. I forced a grateful smile, that didn't quite make it all the way to my adoring blue eyes. "She is very ill at the moment, but she will…" I was prevented from finishing my sentence, by the loud screech of Harriet's mocking, nasal drawl, drifting towards me. "Come along William" she bellowed, in as loud and threatening a voice as possible, surrounded as usual by her

46

cronies. Sensing trouble, the few villagers walking by all stopped talking at once, to turn their heads in Harriet's direction. I felt Hannah take a step towards me once more and switched all my attention onto Harriet, watching her warily. For her part, Harriet was immensely enjoying being the centre of attention, determined to make the delicious feeling of power last as long as possible. The gleam in her eye resembled a cat when it mercilessly tortures a mouse, just for the sheer fun of being in control. Smiling apologetically, William whispered "I don't want her to antagonise you any further, so I'll go, but I'll be seeing you again soon Molly Downer. You can be certain of that." A thrill ran through me at his words. I had heard the clear intent in his voice and was surer than I had ever been, that I would have him as my husband, one way or another. Harriet might have won her small victory for the moment, but I was determined to win the ultimate contest in the end. I would win William Gould and spend the rest of my life flaunting my good fortune in her petulant little face.

"Did you see that ?" Hannah asked me incensed, as we heard the unmistakable sound of Harriet's gloating laughter trailing back towards where we stood, surrounded by a group of onlookers. "She clicked her fingers and he just followed her like a lost dog. He allowed her to make a fool out of you in front of everyone we know."

"I wouldn't worry about it," I smiled knowingly, "I'm going to make him forget all about Harriet Morey, just you see if I don't." Hannah was prevented from commenting further, when my father stepped out of the church and into the harsh sunlight, standing directly behind us. "Well then my dear" he said in his usual, overly bright voice, the one that he always uses whenever we find ourselves together in public. "Did you enjoy the service today ?" Forgetting all about the gorgeous William Gould and the repulsive Harriet Morey in an instant, I was beaming "oh yes, of course I did. I thought you were truly wonderful. I still can't believe that you're going to be here all of the time, the village is truly blessed to have you." A tinge of pink coloured his cheeks in embarrassment, as he looked around to see how many people were trying to listen in on our conversation and realised from the guilty looks he saw, that there were quite a few villagers trying to look innocent as they blatantly eavesdropped. "Are you well ?" He asked, considering me carefully, in the way that he always did when he was concerned about something. "Quite well thank you" I smiled, trying to reassure him, yet feeling like I wasn't fooling him at all. Lowering his voice and clearly uncomfortable, he whispered "and how is your mother ?" Like a cloud had suddenly passed over the sun, I found myself feeling as icy cold as though I'd just been plunged into the ocean and a tingle of apprehension settled itself in the very pit of my stomach. Pushing away my feelings of foreboding, I matched his tone and answered the question, I knew had cost him so much to ask me. "I am sorry to say that Mama is not well at all. I worry for her so, truly I do. I swear by almighty God that I have never known her to be so desperately ill before." My father squeezed my hand as though he wished to lend me his support, but then abruptly drew away, as though I were a snake that had bitten him, rather than his own daughter looking to him for support in a time of need and left me feeling wretched. He scanned the crowd once more and sure enough, several pairs of eyes were watching us. All pretence had been abandoned and everyone now strained to overhear what was being said between us. "I shall pray for her" he said kindly, but once more I felt the heat of shame working its way through my body, seeping into my very bones. "Are you coming to the hog roast ?" I mumbled uncertainly, at a loss for words. "I'm sorry" he shook his head regretfully, "Jane and I are honoured to be having lunch with the Bishop, the Trinity

Board and the other gentlemen who made the building of the new church possible. I must hurry." My father and I said an awkward goodbye, with him promising to see me soon and my heart aching with rejection. I felt Hannah tug forcefully on my arm, pulling me out of my reverie. "Come on we should go and find something to eat, before Harriet Morey consumes the whole of the hog roast, or could that be considered cannibalism ?"

Outside of the Olde Village Inne, a roasted hog had been carved into huge chunks and placed on giant platters atop large trestle tables. Each family had donated something to the feast and there was more than enough on display to feed a whole hungry village for several days. A group of men sat playing instruments and the strains of flutes and banjos travelled on the spring breeze, as clusters of children and some of the older unmarried girls led everyone in the dancing. I scanned the crowd for William, but much to my annoyance I couldn't see him anywhere. Some people had already filtered into the inn and I wondered if he was already in there surrounded by his friends, competing to see who could drink the most ale. Not wanting to seem too eager, I decided that if our paths did cross, I would pretend to be slightly uninterested and let him do all the running. I knew that men preferred it when girls played hard to get and I didn't want to make him feel trapped, until I was sure that I had him in my thrall and although I was confident that I would have him, it was still far too soon to be completely certain. The excitement of thinking about William, the worry about my mother's health and my disappointment that my father could not stay for the celebrations, all served to dampen my spirits and I no longer felt the urge to dance. My appetite had vanished and to my utter dismay I found that I just wanted to run back to my home and hide away. Hannah had known me long enough to know that something was wrong, so she whispered in my ear, "let's leave the others to their hog roast. We should go and check on how your ma is feeling and then you can come to our house and I'll get my ma to fetch us something to eat. How does that sound to you ?" I've often wondered what I would do if I didn't have Hannah Trickett on my side at all times. We had been friends longer than either of us could remember and were more like sisters, except for the fact that we had never shared a crossed word between us. Hannah's father had died when she was still only two years old. George Trickett had been a well liked fishermen in the village, but like so many others who hailed from Bembridge and all the other ports around the island, he had sadly been lost at sea. I believe that our special bond stemmed from the fact that both of us knew what it was like to be brought up without a father and as a result we were fiercely protective of one another, always ready to stick up for one another when the need arose. I turned to look at my friend, with her light brown hair loosely caught up beneath her emerald coloured hat and matching dress which she always wore to church and I hugged her in grateful thanks, for always knowing just the right thing to say.

Allowing myself to be led away from the inn, I wondered with a stirring of excitement how soon it would be, before I saw my handsome William Gould again and just what I would wear when he took me courting. I smiled to myself as I thought of the pleasure that rubbing Harriet's face in my victory, would bring me.

Chapter 2

My mother sat singing happily to herself, as she pounded a large piece of willow bark with her pestle and mortar. She was feeling well for the first time in days and had even managed to venture into our small stillroom of sorts, next to the tiny kitchen area at the back of the cottage. Instead of holding preserves, the table and wooden shelves were heavily laden with jars and flasks of all shapes and sizes, containing a myriad of unguents, poultices, comfrey ointment to soothe itches, syrup of white poppy to soothe and aid sleep and all the remedies that we could ever need. Dried herbs and flowers such as pennyroyal and gromwell to restart a woman's flow, hung in thick bunches from the beams above and scented the air with the heady mix of a meadow on a summer's evening. Beside her, I sat quietly writing out prayers which I would wrap carefully around each one of the small vials of powder that my mother prepared and sold as a cure for removing stubborn warts. It was one of our biggest sellers and we always liked to have a plentiful supply available for neighbours in need. I've always loved the peaceful harmonious days we spent sitting in the sunshine, replenishing our stocks. We had the pittance that my father sent to us on occasion and we still had some of the money that my mother's family had given her, but most of our money was gained through my mother's knowledge, expertise and enterprise and she had single-handedly built up a prosperous business, upon which the whole village relied. Our help was especially important, as Bembridge was practically cut off from the rest of the island, so the inhabitants couldn't rely solely on outside help from the rest of the island. My mother, ably assisted by myself was the only wise woman and midwife in the village of Bembridge and I privately suspected that she had chosen such an occupation, purely to put her at odds with my father. The church made no secret of the fact that it didn't approve of such things and it was yet one more source of conflict between my parents. As a consequence of our good reputation and the efficacy of our homemade cures, my mother and I had been rushed off our feet with an almost endless line of customers at the door, particularly over the last couple of days and business was indeed flourishing. I always did feel a little guilty, knowing that if my mother was happy and business was brisk, it meant that there were lots of friends and neighbours who were suffering. My mother had learned her extensive knowledge of herbs and remedies from a book given to her by my grandmother, who had explained that each woman in the family had passed down her skills and experience for future generations, the line had only become broken when my own grandmother had refused to have anything to do with such matters, leaving my great-grandmother with the task of ensuring the family legacy. My mother had delivered all of the babies in the village for the past fifteen years and had gained a formidable reputation, for safely bringing so many mothers and children through the ordeal of labour and was often called out at all times of the day and night, along with myself. I assisted my mother in all areas of the business, save for the telling of the runes and the other secret ways that she had of helping people. My mother had the gift, but she had always been at pains to keep me away from that side of the business. "People can be quick enough to point the finger when they have a mind to" she had warned me once. "Someone who is your best customer one day, could be the very one that turns around and accuses you of witchcraft the next day, simply because their wife died of childbed fever or even because their crops failed. People always look for someone to blame, when they're scared or can't accept what has happened to them." She had created a world of constant danger, which had wiped away my feelings of security with just a few words and it made me uneasy that although I was not drawn into the darker side of helping our customers, I still feared for my mother's safety whenever a new customer came asking for help. "The witchcraft trials are thankfully at an end now and the villagers have need of us, but I don't want to put you in danger, by teaching you things that you have no business knowing. Always be cautious in your dealings with people, give them no cause to make trouble. When a customer comes in and I give you the nod, leave us in peace and have a care that you do not overhear anything. Follow my advice my girl and all will be well." I had taken her words to heart and had followed her advice to the letter and our business had remained untroubled, prosperous and thankfully free from scandal.

As we sat merrily absorbed in our work, there came a sudden loud banging on the front door of our thatched cottage, which the locals had always referred to as The Hatch, though I had never been able to find out why. My mother abruptly stopped her singing and we eyed one another warily. "I'll go" I said. Most of our customers who came to buy remedies, or my mother's secret mixtures such as love philtres and other darker cures for girls in trouble, came under cover of darkness and quietly rapped on the back door, wishing to remain unnoticed by curious onlookers who might reveal our secrets. When someone made such a racket at the front of the cottage, it normally meant that there was a village woman suffering the agonies of childbirth, in dire need of our services. I opened the door so quickly that Thomas, one of the local fishermen nearly fell straight through the doorway, as he leant to pound on the heavy door once more. Although he was still under thirty years of age, his skin was like brown leather, yet even with such a dark tan, he seemed unusually pale. "It's my Helen" he gasped, "you have to come. The babe is too early and she's in terrible agony, I don't know what to do, she needs help. She's thrashing around and cursing me." I opened my mouth to assure Thomas that we would come right away and found that my mother was already standing behind me with her bag of implements, powders, salves and cooling balms that she always kept on a hook in the little stillroom ready for any emergency. "Lead on Thomas" my mother said, untying the white apron around her waist with her quick, nimble fingers and casting it aside. She readily assumed the role of midwife in command of the birth, even before she had even set a foot outside of her own cottage, it was a force of habit borne out of years of experience. As a fisherman Thomas stood without flinching against the worst storms heaven could hurl down upon him. He had faced great rolling waves almost as high as the chapel itself and had not turned away, yet the very minute that his wife started screaming in pain, his instinct was to run and fetch my mother and I. I honestly don't think that Thomas had ever before felt so helpless and he seemed grateful to be ordered around. Out of his mind with fear, he led us to his small cottage, forgetting that we had been living in the village for eighteen years and were more than capable of finding our way without him. There was little in the way of any belongings inside the fisherman's house and each room contained the all-pervading smell of bass and conger, making my stomach roll, in revulsion. Thomas ushered us into the bedroom, where his wife Helen lay writhing in agony, twisting the blankets absent mindedly as she clenched her fists, trying to brace herself against the terrible pain and her anxiety rose with each fresh onslaught. "It's alright Helen" my mother soothed, "we're here now, everything is going to be alright." Putting the bag down carefully, she approached the bed, "let's have a look and see how far we are from meeting your new baby shall we ?" Safe in the knowledge that his wife was in the best hands possible, Thomas quietly slipped from the room and I just spotted the door gently close, out of the corner of my eye. 'Typical' I thought to myself crossly, 'he's the one who got her this way and he's the one who cannot face the reality of it all. I'd take a wager that he's never moved so fast in his life.' It always irritated me that the man would disappear at the first sign of labour. His wife would go through all the physical stress and the agony of bringing a child into the world, and when it was all over, especially if the child turned out to be a boy, the father would be the first to parade around his new son in public and have no qualms at all in taking all of the credit for producing his offspring. Whenever I complained about the injustice of it all to my mother, she would shrug her shoulders and simply say, "such is the way of the world and such is a woman's lot for her sins in the Garden of Eden. It is as the good Lord God wills it," before squeezing my hand reassuringly. This baby was Helen's first, and as a rule my mother found first time mothers to be the hardest of all to deal with. When a woman had been through childbirth before, she knew what to expect the next time around and knew what was expected of her in return. When a woman didn't know what was going to happen and her head was full of the horror stories from gossiping friends, my mother found it much harder to calm them down and it was consequently more difficult for her to concentrate on the job of getting the baby safely into the world, when the mother was screaming the place down, this was where I came into my own, by keeping the mother as calm as possible, by distracting her as much as possible. As I approached the small iron bed, I pulled up a seat and sat next to Helen, holding her hand which trembled alarmingly as she bestowed a wan smile on me. "I was so scared that Tom wouldn't be able to find you, I'm so glad you're here. Please, please you have to help me. It hurts so much."

My mother was muttering to herself as she examined Helen's distended stomach, gently pressing down on the lower abdomen, making her scream out loud in pain. I could tell from my mother's expression that all was not well, but I knew from experience, not to ask what was wrong. When my mother was ready to speak, she would and she would be careful not to alarm the mother to be. Opening her bag, my mother produced a small jar of lavender and lemon, which she used to wash her hands in a bowl of water, placed on a table near to the end of the bed, carefully covering her hands and wrists thoroughly, before carrying out her examination. Helen twisted in pain, but she tried to be as compliant as possible. Never one to mince her words, my mother believed in honesty being the best policy at all times, especially during childbirth. The villagers admired her forthrightness and the way she took command of any situation, but I alone knew the personal toll it took on her. When she worked, she put her whole heart and soul into everything she did, but she wasn't getting any younger and when we returned home, she would be exhausted. Gently, my mother probed the frightened woman's abdomen and pelvis, trying to ascertain the position of the baby in the womb, grimacing with empathy whenever Helen whimpered or writhed in misery. "Helen, the babe is going to come out arse first, there's no way to turn it and baby is in a hurry to come out. It's not going to be easy I'm afraid. You're going to need to be really brave." Helen shuddered as another wave of pain washed over her. "I can't do this" she panted. "I can't do it."

"Too late for that I'm afraid" said my mother, wishing that she had a shilling for every mother who had declared that they weren't up to the task. "Still now you know what causes it, you can make sure to avoid it from happening again can't you ?" She said with mock sternness and a friendly wink, managing to raise the ghost of a smile on Helen's lips, as she grimaced at the pain. "Don't you worry, it won't be happening again, I can assure you of that and I'll tell that husband of mine the same thing, when next I see him."

"Ah my dear they all say that at first, but once you hold your tiny little babe in your arms, you'll change your mind soon enough, you mark my words." My mother's eyes twinkled good-naturedly as she looked down at the scared fisherman's wife. I winced, as I saw my mother swiftly take her small knife out of the bag and place it behind the bowl of water. The urge to push was becoming more frequent and I tried to keep Helen's fears from taking root and letting her imagination run wild, by focusing her mind on the happy event that was about to take place. "What do you wish for ? A boy or a girl ? And what names have you chosen ?" These were my standard questions and as usual, the mother's sprits rallied whenever her thoughts turned towards her new child. Finding a brief respite in between contractions she managed to answer. "My Tom would love for this baby to be a boy, a son to eventually become a fishermen alongside him. It would make my heart glad to see him happy and so proud, but I would love a daughter, so that I could keep her safely at home with me, rather than fear every day that they are out on the cruel sea together. If it's a boy we shall name him Thomas for his father and grandfather and if it's a girl, then she is to be called Mary after my mother." The contractions began to increase in intensity and Helen lost her ability to speak. I whispered soothingly, "pretend you are out on the sea in Thomas' boat and coming towards you are high waves. With each swell, concentrate on guiding the boat over the crest of it and down to the other side, then gather your strength in the lull before the next one comes along. You can do this! When it's all over, you'll be so very glad that you did. I promise you."

Cautiously, I eyed Helen, who had thankfully become quieter under my calming guidance. Her eyes were closed and she was panting her way through the spasms of pain that were almost constant in their assault. "Right, this one's ready to be born, so when I tell you, I am going to need you to push." Helen nodded imperceptibly, her hair stuck to her skin and sweat was trickling constantly down her face. Her energy had almost evaporated, leaving her looking tired and exhausted, but she gritted her teeth, ready to do as my mother told her. "The babe is coming quickly for a first child, so brace yourself my dear and .... Push." Helen pushed with all her might. I held onto her hand and watched with a grimace, as my mother made a swift cut with her knife allowing the baby easier passage. Screaming out in pain, Helen squeezed my hand with the last remainder of her energy, reminding me why I had decided to never have children myself. The legs emerged first, along with a perfectly formed, yet miniature pair of buttocks and slowly, the waist became visible. Helen lay, as white as a sheet upon the bed, her power spent, yet her job still only half done. "Push again," ordered my mother briskly, holding the cord in her left hand. Helen grunted as the shoulders were freed and the head was slowly eased through the birth canal. Too often I had seen babies born the wrong way around, suffocating before they could be safely brought into the world, but after a tense moment of silence we were rewarded with a lustily squalling infant, whose forceful bellows filled the room. My mother cleaned the outraged infant, wrapping him safely in a blanket before handing him over to his exhausted mother, who looked at him as though he were the first baby ever to be born to a woman. "Congratulations my dear, you have a fine baby boy."

I assisted with the delivery of the afterbirth, watching in awe as my mother deftly sewed neat stitches into the cut she had made. Helen didn't even seem to notice the pain, as she steadily gazed at her newborn child. Once her nightdress and the bloodstained bedding had been changed, I went to seek out Thomas. I did not have far to look, he was leaning up against the wall of the cottage. "Is... is everything OK ?" He asked and my heart filled with compassion at the pleading tone in his voice. Helen was his whole world and if he lost her, he lost everything. "Mother and babe are both fine, baby gave us a fright by coming out legs first, but all is well. You have a very brave wife, you should be proud of her."

"Oh I am," he beamed in delight. "Is it a boy or a girl ?" I could see his face draining of all colour, as the realisation that he was now a father hit him. "I think after all of her hard work, it should be your wife that gives you the news." I laughed and motioned him into the bedroom, where Helen sat with the contented glow of a new mother, gazing in wonder at the child in her arms.

I fetched some warm water for washing our hands and once we'd packed up all of our belongings, we crept to the side of the bed where the baby lay feeding. His owlish eyes swept the room, taking everything in, before considering his parents with a solemn expression, making his father chuckle. "Come and say hello to my son, Thomas Henry Bull" Tom whispered, his wife smiling drowsily at his enthusiasm. Thomas had lost his own father in a storm at sea, when Thomas was still only a ten year old boy and the whole village had felt the family's grief. It was a fitting tribute and old Thomas would have been very proud of his fine new grandson. "That's a big name for such a small lad" my mother nodded, "but I think he'll grow into it just fine. We'll leave you all in peace. Just come and find us if there is anything you need and I'll pop in tomorrow morning with a tisane to see how you are." As we left, Thomas pressed us to take our usual fee of four shillings, along with armfuls of fresh and dried fish and a large bottle of brandy that would last us for at least a month. We accepted the gifts along with his repeated thanks for safely delivering his son, the next one in a long line of fishermen. "I have been delivering the babies in this village for nearly as long as you've been alive" my mother laughed, as we trudged slowly back to our home, carrying bundles of fish, "yet I don't believe that I have ever seen a new father as proud as Thomas Bull is of that little boy."

Chapter 3

"Where are you off to in such a hurry young lady ?" My
mother croaked at me, peaking around the heavy curtains.
For the past week, she had been too ill to stir from her bed,
unable to venture down the stairs which left me with much
to do. "We are in need of some more rabbit, butter and
milk and then I have to dig up some vegetables and collect
some eggs from out back, why ?" I tried my level best to
smooth my features into an innocent expression, but to my
great annoyance I found the corners of my mouth twitching
involuntarily. My mother's body was certainly ailing, but
her mind was still as sharp as a mason's chisel. She
watched me intently, as I danced around the room, in my
green dress and matching bonnet. "Don't try and pretend to
me that you are just going to fetch rabbit, digging up
vegetables or chasing after the chickens in that dress. You
are dressed in all your finery. You look as though you're
ready to go and pray in church, not to collect some butter."
Realising that I had no choice but to tell her the truth, or
else I would never be trusted out of the house again, I fell
backwards onto her bed, narrowly missing her frail legs. "I
actually do have to buy all of those things and I do need to
work outside, but if you want me to be truthful, I was
hoping that I would see William Gould whilst I was out."
My mother was silent for a moment as she tried to
remember which of the village boys, William was. She had
never known me to show special interest in a boy, let alone
glow at the mere mention of a name. "Do you mean
Kathryn Gould's grandson ? That skinny young lad who
moved to the village from Sandown ?" I was never any
good at being teased, especially by my mother and pouted

at her crossly. "Yes that is William, but he's not a skinny young lad anymore. He's a shipbuilder now and you should see his muscles when he rolls his shirt sleeves up. He really is the handsomest boy in the village and I plan to win him." "Well" she said with a chuckle. "If there's one thing I can be certain of, it's that if you have finally set your cap at a boy, then he stands absolutely no chance of escaping. Go out, have a good time, but watch that you don't get yourself a reputation my girl." Uncertain whether I could wholeheartedly keep the promise to protect my reputation if the time came, I happily skipped out of the room and down the old creaking stairs. My mother was asleep before I even closed the front door quietly behind me.

It was late in the morning and as usual the village was full with mothers and their young children. Dogs chased squawking chickens around in the dust, getting under the feet of anyone who tried to walk by. The fields stretched right up to the High Street and as far as the eye could see, there were men working hard in the already humid morning. Carts trundled precariously past me and a young mason's apprentice tipped his hat giving me a cheeky wink as he and his master walked by, boosting my confidence for finding and enticing William Gould. I was satisfied that I had never looked more beautiful and it gave me a spring in my step. I had never thought of these mundane sights as remarkable before, but for the first time ever, I felt as though the whole village was bathed in a heavenly golden glow. The simplest of things made my heart leap with joy and whilst I took everything in, I was constantly on the alert for William Gould.

Walking as slowly as I could through the village, I made the time to stop and talk to anyone who caught my eye, so that I could dawdle for longer in an effort to find my beloved. My conscience told me that I should go home, that my mother would be wondering where I was, but I convinced myself that my mother was probably still asleep and I might disturb her slumber, if I was selfish and returned home too soon. Once my purchases had been made and I'd stopped to talk with anyone and everyone I could find, I reluctantly headed back in the direction of The Hatch. My bursting optimism had completely dissipated and after building up my expectations higher than the spire of the St Mary's Church, I felt the disappointment even more keenly. The basket was weighing heavily on my tired arm and my head drooped despondently as I stared dully at the rocks and earth beneath my feet. Nearing the cottage, a familiar voice broke into my thoughts, making me whip my head around in excited disbelief. I had spent the whole morning dawdling around the village, only for William Gould to appear before me at my front door. "Good morning Mol. I was just coming to seek you out." Instantly, my mood was transformed. I smiled in my most alluring way, fluttering my eyelashes prettily, a little trick I've used ever since I found that boys respond best to flattery. "Why ever would you be looking for me ?" I asked, pretending a wide eyed innocence that was fooling no one, least of all myself. "I wanted to know if your ma could make a love potion for me ?" His reply was totally unexpected, rendering me temporarily speechless, giving William the chance to grab my hand in both of his, holding me in place, staring at me intently. "I want to make you fall hopelessly in love with me Molly Downer. Do you think your mother has anything in that back room of hers that could possibly make you desire me ?"

Drawing him towards the side of the house, where we were less likely to be seen or overheard, I allowed him to hold my hand. Forcing myself to meet his gaze, I felt the same pleasing warmth running throughout the length of my body, as it did whenever I drank brandy. "My ma doesn't make potions like that and well you know it William

Gould" I halfheartedly admonished him, "I think that perhaps I might be the one to help you though, all the same." Watching him closely, I waited for his reply. William pushed his hair out of his eyes and I noticed that his shirt sleeves were once again rolled up to display his bulging muscles to impressive effect and my knees felt weak with desire. Raising my hand to his lips, I shuddered as his warm dry lips pressed against my cool skin. "I have some free time this afternoon, please say you can escape and come for a walk with me." My mother's warning not to ruin my reputation, ran briefly through my mind, but I quickly cast my doubts aside, took a deep breath and nodded. "I can... I would love to, thank you." Pleased at my response and with promises of calling back for me, he let go of my hand and raced off in the direction of the shipyard. I stood watching him, until I could no longer make out his white shirt, his deep brown woollen waistcoat and coarse brown trousers and I prided myself that there was no boy as fine in the whole village than my William.

Closing the door quietly behind me, I placed my basket down carefully on the table, crept as quietly as I could up the stairs and slowly opened the door to my mother's room. At first I thought she was still sleeping and I'd gotten away with being out for so long, but as usual, my mother was as sharp as a needle. "Who were you talking to outside ? Was it your beau ?" Walking around to the side of the bed, where she lay, I saw that her gaze lay on some daffodils, one of the neighbours had obviously brought for her, in a jug near the window. "I was talking to Joe from the forge" I lied smoothly, surprised at how easily the falsehood had risen to my lips, but I could not risk rousing my mother's suspicions. "His wife is due to have her baby soon and he needed some reassurance. Anyway I want to know how you are."

"Oh" she replied truculently. "You've suddenly remembered me now, have you ?" Whenever my mother was ill, all the responsibility and work fell upon my shoulders, so I resented the fact that my mother begrudged me time to go and buy provisions, or to have any freedom whatsoever. How else was I supposed to find myself a husband, if I was forced to remain indoors, looking after an elderly mother confined to her bed ? I bit my lip before I could utter something I would later regret and leapt to my feet. "I'll make us something to eat." By the time I had dug some carrots and potatoes from the patch and cooked them along with the rabbit, my temper had thankfully mellowed. My body tingled in anticipation as I thought of my impending secret meeting with William and how furious my mother would be if she ever found out that I had slipped away to be alone with a boy.

The last few weeks had been particularly tiresome and I decided that it was time to have some much deserved enjoyment. Feeling much calmer, I helped my mother to sit up in the bed and slowly fed her small chunks of the meat and vegetables. I was impatient to get away, but I smoothed my features, hiding my irritation and bolting down my own food with one hand, whilst I fed my mother with the other, attempting to make small talk about the weather outside. The yellow rays of the sun poured in through the window, bathing us in its golden warmth. We talked for a while about how the pigs fared and how many customers had called whilst I was out. I noted with relief that my mother had finally closed her eyes once more and snored lightly in her sleep. Quietly, I took the remains of our meal downstairs, placing them on the side to be cleaned later. Brushing the creases out of my gown and smoothing my hair neatly into place, I hurried around the cottage.

Carefully, I banked up the fire once more. It had started to turn cold in the late afternoons as the nights began to start drawing in and I didn't want my mother to wake simply because of the chill and find that I had left her alone once more. Creeping as quiet as a mouse, I checked that she was still fast asleep, before tiptoeing back downstairs to wait for William. Picking up a blouse with a ripped sleeve with the intention of repairing it, I found that I couldn't concentrate and instead spent the time like a dog watching for its master's return. There weren't as many people around and so I spotted him immediately as he walked right up to the cottage, slipping around the back out of sight. I was at the back door, before he had even reached it, then silently cursed myself for seeming too eager. He took off his soft floppy cap and affected an elaborate bow as though I were a queen of the blood royal. "Shall we ?" He offered me his arm and giggling at his bright humour, I accepted, allowing him to lead me off, skirting around Steyne's Copse until we reached the old windmill belonging to the Dennetts. "What's in your bag ?" I asked, wondering if he had decided to go poaching on the way home. "You'll find out" he replied mysteriously. We continued up the hill, talking about the weather and asking politely after each other's families. I was relieved that our conversations were on safe subjects, my heart was already beating so alarmingly in excitement that I didn't think that I could stand much more. I luxuriated in the deliciousness of our secret assignation, but underneath my daring and desire, I was still a good God fearing daughter of a Reverend and I knew that I wouldn't let things go too far. I also knew that the secret to keeping a man interested was the promise of what was to come, if I seemed too loose with my morals now, William might not think of me as suitable marriage material and that couldn't be allowed to happen.

Without realising it, William had brought me to one of my favourite places. The mill had been standing silently, at the top of the hill overlooking Bembridge for at least eight years and I always found it a peaceful spot to sit and think, away from the constant prying eyes of the rest of the village. The sails were barely moving, there wasn't a breath of wind across the whole island and I wished that I'd thought to bring a drink with me, after our energetic walk. William led me across to a dense grove of trees, where we sat in the welcome shade to cool down. Reaching into his bag, he produced a bottle of honey mead and two wooden cups. "I thought we might need these," he smiled smugly, pulling out the stopper with his teeth. Relieved, I held up my cup allowing him to pour a generous measure of the golden liquid into it. "Why did you bring me to this particular spot ?" I asked, uncertain of whether I wanted to hear the honest answer, scared that he would tell me that this was the place where he brought all of the girls he'd courted. "I passed this spot the other day and thought it would be a good place for us to get to know one another, without any distractions." My hands shook and I drank too much of the syrupy mead far too quickly, coughing at the burning sensation rising in my throat. The shadows lengthened as the sun passed on its slow journey overhead, whilst we talked and drank, until the bottle of mead was empty. I learned that William had been a shipbuilder in the family business for almost three months, he had moved along the coast from Sandown, where there was much less work to be had, to try his luck in Bembridge. I found him easy going and listened intently, clapping my hands in delight as he talked to me of the trouble that he and his brothers got into, playing practical jokes on their poor beleaguered mother. For my part, I related the tale of how my father and mother had met and of the wealthy family that she had been forced to leave behind. I told him all about the details of my feud with Harriet Morey, how it had all started and I hoped it meant that he would no longer talk to my arch enemy, now that he knew the truth about her and how evil she really was.

The effects of the mead made me feel woozy, but being alone with someone so handsome, I knew I had to keep my wits about me, or else I could be very easily led into trouble. In a general lull in the conversation, we lay back on the cool grass, looking at the clouds passing silently above us and for a while we were content, just trying to find shapes in the soft white clouds. I pointed out one that looked like a sheep, but William didn't reply. I thought perhaps he'd drifted off to sleep in the afternoon heat, so shading my eyes against the sun, I turned towards him and realised that he was no longer lying on his back beside me, but was propping himself up on one arm, looking at me in much the same way that a fox would regard a chicken that had strayed out of its coop. Despite my earlier fears, I found that I was all too willing for him to kiss me, closing my eyes and parting my lips, as he leant in towards me. The kiss was everything that I had dreamt it would be and it frightened me as much as it made me happy. His lips were soft and warm and the pressure behind them was insistent. William slid his tongue into my mouth and I felt an explosion of sensation like no other. Next came the novel sensation of heat and the weight of his body on top of me, he crushed all the resistance out of my body.

Just as I was about to be pushed to the point of no return, we heard footsteps walking through the long grass, directly towards our hiding place. William instantly jumped up as though he had been scolded and I hid myself behind one of the trees, my heart pounding in my chest in fear. Peeking around the rough trunk, I saw that it was young Albert, one of the lads who worked at the mill alongside the new head miller William Fowles. The lack of wind had obviously meant that the mill had been abandoned for the day and the workers would all be passing by on their way back to the village. Albert looked like a ghost, he was covered from top to toe in a fine white powder and suffered from a persistent cough, making his small frame shake mercilessly. "William," he said with a knowing wink and without even breaking his stride he shouted, "afternoon Molly." I had just begun to think I had gotten away without being seen and the crippling embarrassment left me momentarily paralysed. Frantically, I rearranged my dress and the strands of hair which had worked their way loose. I soon realised that I would never look as presentable as I had when I left the cottage and gave up my futile efforts. The sun was beginning to slowly descend in the sky and I realised with alarm how late I was, how close I had come to total ruin and that being spotted by Albert in such a compromising position, might actually have done the very thing that my mother had implicitly warned me not to do. If Albert told anyone that I had been alone with William in a field looking dishevelled, my reputation would be tarnished forever. "I must go." I hardly dared to glance at William, as I rushed past, unwilling to give him the chance to stop me, embarrassed at how far I had let him go.

I was halfway back to the cottage before he managed to catch up with me. He had stopped to pick up the bag, the cups and the empty bottle before chasing after me and I had been eager to get as far away from him as possible. "Hey Mol wait up will you. What's the hurry ?" William grabbed my arm, preventing me from marching away from him. "Albert won't say anything to anyone, trust me. I've turned a blind eye to that boy's scrapes many a time, he owes me a little discretion." His words had the desired effect and I visibly relaxed, even managing to give him a shaky smile. "Can I see you again ?" He asked, taking as took a step towards me. I nodded slowly even though my mind was screaming at me to run in the other direction as fast as possible. I closed my eyes, as he kissed me once again. "I'll see you soon," were his last words, as he disappeared in the direction of his uncle's house. I stood watching him in mute silence, with the taste of him still on my lips, my heart pounding wildly and my mind in a whirl.

The minute that I walked in through the door, I knew I had stayed away from home for too long and wracked my brain for an excuse that my mother would find plausible. "Molly is that you ?" Came her reedy voice from above. I had managed to throw off my responsibilities for a short time, but when faced with reality, I felt ashamed. I had let my mother down and not been there for her, for most of the day, yet I felt torn. I couldn't blame William for his advances, I had wanted him to kiss me and would have most likely have let things go farther if Albert hadn't made his appearance when he did. "Yes it's me ma, I'm sorry I'm so late. Shall I bring you up a cup of tea ?"

Handing over the cup of steaming liquid, I seated myself gently on the side of the bed. "Where have you been for all this time ? I hope you haven't been walking up and down all day, waiting to ensnare your young man." The sun had sunk low in the sky and night would be swift to follow. Whilst I had been making the tea, I had decided that there would be no point in trying to deny how long I had been missing from home, my mother's ailments were only physical and she was too shrewd to be fooled, so I decided to lie about where I'd been instead. "I went to see Hannah and I thought that you would be asleep. I'm really so very sorry for being gone so long. I should have come back earlier, but we were busy talking and I forgot myself." I felt a pang of guilt, as I saw just how tired my mother looked. The rims around her eyes were pink and sore, despite the amount of time she'd spent asleep in the past few days.

With apprehension, I saw how much effort it took for her just to sit up. "Did you have a good time at Hannah's ?" "Yes. Why don't you rest and I'll go and make us something to eat, then afterwards we could read some of your psalms. How does that sound ?" To make up for my afternoons transgressions, I sat with my mother and told her all of the latest gossip. The talk of one of the young village farm hands who'd recently got one of the local dairy maids pregnant and then disappeared, wasn't as enjoyable in the retelling as I had thought it earlier however. As my mother began to tire out, I sang her favourite hymns softly under my breath and embroidered until my eyes burned with the effort.

Once she had finally fallen asleep for the evening, I crept downstairs and swept the floor, cleaned the plates and took the food scraps outside for the very grateful pigs. Yawning loudly, I grabbed the candle, my eyelids were beginning to droop and I was consumed with exhaustion. I'd just started up the stairs when I heard a soft rapping on the back door.

Due to our proficiency in curing people, we often find customers knocking on our back door at all hours. At night time, there was much less chance of a customer being noticed by the rest of the village and the rear of The Hatch was helpfully obscured from view by overgrown trees and hedges, set at a convenient angle so as not to be overlooked by any neighbours. With the small candleholder firmly in my hand, I swung open the door expecting a customer in need, but instead I found myself face to face with my beloved William. "Molly" he whispered, checking behind himself to ensure that we weren't being overheard. "When can you slip away again ?" I'd spent all evening feeling guilty for my assignation with him and although I knew that it should never happen again, I couldn't prevent my desire to go with him all the same. I thought of my mother safely asleep above us and what she would say if she knew what had passed between us and that William was obviously back to make certain that it definitely would happen again. I shook my head of all common sense and warnings and whispered back saucily, "why, what did you have in mind?"

His wicked grin and the twinkle in his eyes were infectious, making me feel reckless, but the excitement was mounting and it was too late for me to turn back. I prayed that he wanted to see me again as soon as possible. "I have to go away for a few weeks..." His unexpected words sent me into a panic and I gasped in pain at the thought of being parted from him so soon. "I'll be with my dad and uncle, we've got some work in East Cowes that could earn us a lot of money. I just wanted to see you one last time before we leave. Can you meet me an hour before sun up, in the morning?" Too excited to speak I simply nodded, allowing him to kiss me once again with his warm, sensual lips, just briefly, before he ran off, melting into the darkness like a spirit. Slowly closing the door, I crept hurriedly to my room. No matter how exhausted I might have been only moments ago, I was convinced that sleep would prove elusive for me after so much excitement and disappointment, so late at night.

The hours ticked by so slowly as I lay in my bed, waiting for the morning to arrive. Irritably, I finally accepted that I was never going to sleep, so I dressed with care, before quietly pouring water from a pitcher into a basin and washed my face, trying to make as little noise as possible. Brushing my hair until it shone like silk, I arranged it carefully over my shoulders and once I was pleased with the effect, I waited. The sky was still dark and gloomy outside the cottage, when I pushed back the curtains and saw William waiting for me, just as he had promised he would. The chickens and pigs were still sleeping soundly as we crept away from the cottage in silence. Hugging my shawl tightly to me, I shuddered. I had deliberately chosen to wear my thickest dress for warmth, but the air still felt cool on my cheeks and I shivered uncontrollably, wondering for the hundredth time if I was doing the right thing.

Once we were safely away from the village and prying eyes, William took my hand. "Where are we going ?" I asked, eyeing the old brown bag slung casually over one shoulder. "I want you to see something special, to make a memory for us to hold onto whilst we are apart for heaven knows how long." Intrigued, I happily allowed him to lead me along the main road, until he suddenly turned left and made our way through How's Copse. Lost in my own thoughts of the future, I gasped when suddenly the sea breeze assaulted my senses and we found ourselves overlooking the golden sand of the beach. William helped me to negotiate the uneven surface as we passed from the grassy tufts and clambered down under the overhanging dunes. Taking a blanket out of his bag, William motioned for me to sit and I wondered why he had brought me to sit in the cold dark dunes and cursed the fact that after catching a chill, I would most probably end up with a fever and be just as incapacitated as my mother, which wouldn't be of much use to us or the village. I was about to object, when he slipped his arm around me, and I began to feel the warmth from his body spreading throughout mine, making my heart sing in response. Instinctively, I sank into him and fervently hoped that this time, no one would find us in our hiding place. The top of the dune above us, provided a little shelter and snuggling up against William, I felt content. In the years since I had discovered boys, I had enjoyed the attention and although I liked them well enough and I knew they liked me, I had never seemed able to find the right one. My mother had made her own way in life, albeit partly with finances from her family, but growing up in that environment, I was reluctant to hand over my freedom in exchange for being tied down to a man. As my mother's assistant I had also seen at first hand, the downside of love. The girls who were desperate for a potion to make the object of their desire fall madly in love with them, more often than not, once they had caught their chosen one, they came to The Hatch wanting to find a way out of the trouble they'd found themselves in. The ones who had lost their loves were the worst to deal with, they were out of their minds with the pain, which all left me very guarded when it came to the 'L' word, but with William Gould, it just felt right and I knew I'd finally found the one young man that I was ready to hand over my freedom, my heart and my innocence to. William had something which set him above all others, he was as special and out of place amongst the village boys, as a rose amongst a meadow of weeds. "This is what I brought you here to see, look at that sunrise, isn't it beautiful ?" He whispered, breaking into my private thoughts. Staring across the grey green water, I saw the sun just beginning to emerge and watched speechless as the glowing orb made the beginning of its journey across the expanse of sky opening up in front of us. The thin clouds were highlighted with a golden hue, making them look as though they had been set aflame. The sky above us was a riot of blues, making me certain that God himself must have swept those bright gold and yellow ribbons of colour, across the sky with a giant brush, surely only his hand could have accomplished something so beautiful. There was a distinctly rosy glow, edging the blue and I pushed away the notion that a storm was coming, how could I ruin the moment with worry and superstition. "It's beautiful" I breathed. Due to the nature of our work, my mother and I had always kept late hours, sleeping in until well after sunrise and we never had time to dawdle at the water's edge, so this this was a sight I wasn't used to and the result was breathtaking. William produced some cold cuts of gammon, a small loaf of bread and a large bottle of cider with a flourish. As the waves washed noisily against the shore and the small fishing boats looked like dots bobbing along on the water, we finished our food in silence, watching the beauty of the morning unfolding before our eyes.

The morning light grew brighter every moment, yet with the dune at our backs and the empty beach in front of us, we felt perfectly secluded, wrapped up in each other's company. William ran his rough calloused hands over my shoulders, before running them gently up my neck, making me shiver in delicious anticipation, as he leant towards me and our lips met, once more, I felt an explosion of sensation. His tongue slipped into my mouth and a part of me told me that I should be protesting, but all that I could manage was a loud groan of pleasure. William's kisses gradually became more insistent and as he leaned in ever closer I found myself powerless to resist. I didn't even realise that I was being slowly pushed backwards until I lay flat on by back with the sheet underneath me. His hands stroked my throat and he swallowed hard, "oh God I want you Mol, I'm crazy with love for you. You do know that do you not ?" As he quickly undid the buttons at the neck of my blouse, slipping his hand inside, his thumb lightly brushed against my nipple and I felt my mind unravel.

"This is where they put in last time," came a man's booming voice, directly overhead but just out of sight. I jumped in fright and William leapt away from me, smoothing his hair down. He held his finger to his lips and I hardly dared to breathe as we waited in silence. "It's alright," William whispered, peering over the edge of the dune that had thankfully concealed us from view. "It was just the revenue men. They're after smugglers, not lovers.

They've gone, they didn't see us." Each time that I had found myself alone with him, we had been disturbed and I started to seriously wonder whether these close calls might be a sign from God, that I should keep my virtue intact, at least until the wedding day, rather than being so voluntarily wanton at every given opportunity. "I'm sorry William, but I have to go. My ma's still sick, she'll be wondering where I am, especially when she's so suspicious about where I was yesterday." Once the heat of temptation had passed and the chill of reality began to dawn on me, I found that I couldn't even bring myself to look at him any longer and my cheeks were aflame with embarrassment. "Fine," William seemed unusually brusque and didn't reach out to offer me his hand as we walked rapidly back towards my home, even when we passed through the dense copse and I peeked frantically around us in the darkness between the trees. As the silence engulfed me, I became lost in my own thoughts. I told myself that William was acting differently because the hour was now late and there were going to be more people around to see us and by lunchtime we would surely be the main point of gossip for the whole village. I kept reminding myself that I hadn't imagined those words, he had said that he loved me and I calmed myself with the certain knowledge that the next obvious step would be for him to speak to my father to arrange our marriage.

As we walked, his stride became shorter and William suddenly began talking about the importance to his family's business of the new work they'd secured in East Cowes and how he would be gone from the village for a few weeks at least, depending on how much progress they made. "I will miss you though, dearest sweet Mol," he said more brightly, "I will come and find you as soon as I get back home, be in no doubt about that." Deciding that I would have to talk to him now, or else drive myself mad over the next few days, wishing that I had been brave enough to tell him how I felt. I came to an abrupt stop. Reaching out I grabbed his hand and he watched me expectantly. I fought to find courage, but what little I could muster disappeared when I looked into his eyes. "William, I... I."

"Go on" he nodded, squeezing my hand reassuringly.

"I fear that I may have given you the wrong impression back there in the dunes. I do love you, with all my heart, but I'm the daughter of a man of God, I simply cannot... give myself to you, until... until we are wed. I can't make the same mistake my parents did and live the rest of my life in shame. I want to be an honourable married woman." The silence seemed to last a lifetime, almost deafening in its awkwardness. Tears welled in my eyes, threatening to spill over onto my hot cheeks. I had dared to speak my hopes for the future out loud and let him know that I wished to leave the taint of illegitimacy behind me and all the time he was silent, just staring at me, while I shivered awkwardly in front of him. "I'm glad that you told me Mol," he said at last, "more grateful than you could ever know. I'm sorry that I got so carried away by my feelings for you. Please think no more of it." He kissed me chastely on the cheek and hugged me, when we finally reached my door. "Good bye William. I shall miss you every day." He blew me a kiss and turning the corner, was gone from my sight. Feeling unsatisfied, uneasy and guilty, I decided to go to church. I wanted to pray for forgiveness and if my mother asked where I'd been, I could give her an honest answer, one that she would hopefully be pleased to hear.

Chapter 4

Despite being utterly distraught that my beloved William was far away in Cowes, I still managed to feel excited about the Brading fair. It was only just beginning to get light outside my curtains when I heard Hannah knocking softly on the front door and I ran excitedly out to greet her, enfolding her in a tight hug, my pain momentarily forgotten. Walking along, whispering eagerly to one another, we were joined by more and more people, until almost the whole of the village walked amiably together, before coming to a stop as we waited for the horse boat to carry us across the water to the other side. Last night there had been a riot of pinks and reds streaking across the sky at the setting of the sun and I had gone to sleep happy, knowing it meant that the weather would be fine for the fair.

I watched children skipping beside their mothers, too excited to merely walk, eager to get to the fair as quickly as possible and getting frustrated by their parents lagging behind. I remembered when I had felt the same as them and now I longed for children of my own. Men smoked their pipes and talked about the amount of fish they had caught this week or how particularly fine the latest batch of ale is at the Olde Village Inne tasted and I watched it all with a detached air. Women prattled about the latest village scandals, young men bragged about winning competitions at the fair and we older girls stared into the distance, dreaming of the colourful ribbons we planned to buy. Brading was an exciting town for us Bembridge residents at the best of times. It always seemed so bustling and vibrant compared to our small little village, but the day of the fair was the most exciting time of the year, when Brading was transformed into a colourful, magical wonderland, just for one day. Traders from Newport brought their goods and there were always so many delights on offer, I thought I would burst from excitement if we didn't get there soon.

Hannah and I clambered onto the horse boat and sitting side by side, we held onto our hats, watching the ribbons flowing in the light breeze behind us. The villagers were indeed a sight to behold. Everyone had made an effort, dressed as they were in their finery. On fairs and holiday days, they brought out clothes that rarely saw the light of day and were reserved for these special occasions only, no one wanted the Brading inhabitants to look down their noses at us. The fashions were mostly out of date and some were decades old, but they had been lovingly protected and were proudly worn. Hannah and I had been saving our money for months and the coins jangled pleasingly beneath our skirts as we walked slowly around the stalls, determined to savour the pleasure of every minute. A cool breeze stopped us from becoming overly hot and music played as we looked around at the vast array of wares on offer, eager to spend our hard earned money. Stopping at one stall filled with dark gingerbread, we allowed the young vendor to flatter us into each buying a piece each. I sighed as my throat was warmed by the slight peppery taste and idly wondered whether I should buy some more. Fortified with our tasty treat, we walked on through the rows of stalls. The noise of the vendors vying with each other for custom and the chatter of the prospective buyers haggling over the cost was deafening, but all part of the Brading experience and I wished that my mother could have been here with me. Surveying the huge array of fruit, nuts and sweetmeats in front of us, we only stopped to buy some ale to quench our thirsts. Before long, we found a stall selling ribbons of all the colours of the rainbow. I purchased a length of light blue ribbon which perfectly matched the colour of my eyes and a length of deep forest green to trim my new hat. Hannah was normally hesitant at spending money, but today she chose several different colours and when I judged that the time was right, I determined to ask her why she was indulging in so many fripperies, but felt wrong to enquire on such a day of happiness. Hannah usually told me all her secrets when she was ready anyway and I hoped that she would confide in me before too long.

As the morning wore on, our stomachs began to grumble loudly in protest. Stopping briefly at the nearest stall, we saw row upon row of pies, their golden pastry shining in the sun and the gravy that had spilt down the side, made them look far too delicious to pass up. Hannah and I chose ones which contained succulent chunks of lamb and soft potato and wiping the warm gravy from our chins, we walked towards where crowds of people had gathered in front of an open air circus ring. Not so long ago, there would have been an angry snorting bull tied to the heavy iron ring in the centre of the town, being attacked by snarling dogs. Bets were taken, wagers won and lost and finally, when it was all over and the dogs had succeeded in killing the tethered beast, there would be a huge feast and the delicious meat would be devoured by the grateful crowd. Sadly the ring lay empty today. My mother had told me that recently a man called George Bull from West Cowes had been prosecuted for baiting a bull and so it had quickly become a practice that was no longer popular with the masses and as a consequence the circus had been needed to offer an added spectacle.

The circus master stood grandly in the middle of the ring, announcing that we were to be treated to acts of acrobatic daring, comedic clowning, dangerous wild animals, rope dancing and dazzling performances on horseback no less. Watching entranced, as I finished off the last morsel of pie, I loved the exotic performances and relished the brightly painted carriages. I had never seen anything so spectacular in all my life and once again I wished that my mother had been well enough to see it for herself, it might be a sight we would never see again and far more exciting than seeing a bull torn apart by hounds. "I'm just going to run back and purchase some more of those lovely ribbons before we leave," Hannah whispered in my ear, rushing off before I could make a reply, although I was secretly pleased that I didn't have to miss a minute of the show. Turning back towards the ring, I felt someone nudging me in the ribs. "Hello young Molly. Are you enjoying yourself ?" I tore my eyes reluctantly away from two jugglers, annoyed at being interrupted, but smiled broadly when I saw it was Lucy Conway demanding my attention. Lucy was also from Bembridge and I had known her for as long as I could remember. My mother and Lucy had been friends ever since she had first moved into the village and she had always been a frequent visitor to The Hatch, seeking my mother out for nothing other than friendship, when the rest of the village only thought of their own needs. "I'm having a lovely time and it's such a perfect day for it" smiling I wolfed down the last morsel of pie. "Are you here alone ?" Lucy asked concerned, looking around to see who my companion might be.

"I'm here with Hannah, she's just gone to get herself even more ribbons. She better not be too long or else she'll miss the jugglers."

"Well" said Lucy, clearly relieved that I wasn't alone. "Give my regards to your mother my dear, I shall call on her tomorrow and fill her in on all the gossip." Grabbing my hand, she pressed three shillings into it, refusing to listen to my protestations that it was far too much money.

Lucy gave me a hug and went on her way, with an empty basket that she meant to fill with goods. I looked down at the shillings in my palm and smiled excitedly, I was determined to spend them, before my mother could find out and disapprove at me taking money from Lucy Conway and insist that I return it. Lucy and her equally kind hearted husband had never been blessed with children of their own and she had always indulged me with little treats every now and again and if it gave her some pleasure, then I found no problem in accepting the gifts, despite my mother's disapproving looks.

The jugglers finished their act and were rewarded with a delighted round of applause, whilst a hat was passed around for donations and jangled with coins by the time it was passed back to the satisfied Circus Master. For a short while, I was entranced by the limber acrobats holding themselves up by one hand, as they travelled upside down on the backs of magnificent silvery white horses, however I eventually began to feel concerned about Hannah, she had been missing for a while and I was starting to feel an uneasy prickling at the nape of my neck. I wasn't certain which direction she'd gone in and didn't want to move from my spot, in case we missed each other, which would be remarkably easy in the tightly packed throng. I told myself that Hannah had simply caught up with her mother and was no doubt finding it hard to get away from her endless prattling. "Here I am!" Announced Hannah, throwing her arms around me. "Where have you been ?" I questioned, feeling aggrieved at being left on my own for so long. "I saw my mother" Hannah said, rolling her eyes and pulling a face. "She wanted to show me everything she'd bought and then pressed me to share a drink with her. I'm sorry Mol, here I got you one of these to show how sincere I am." Passing over a cake, dripping in honey, Hannah linked her arm through mine and we watched the entertainment, my bad mood quite forgotten, as I munched on my treat.

When hunger and thirst made it impossible for us to watch the acts any longer, we followed the aromas blowing tantalisingly on the breeze, until we found our way to the hog roast. It took a while to be served as the roast had proved as popular as always, but the long wait proved to be worth it. I licked my lips as the warm succulent pork fat trickled slowly down my chin, whilst Hannah idly chewed on a hard piece of crackling. "What would you like to do now ?" I asked. The day had been long and in the sweltering heat, I felt myself overcome with fatigue. "We should go and watch the end of the shin kicking contest, before we go for the horse boat." Hannah's decision seemed so forcefully given, that I simply nodded in mute agreement and we went to watch the annual contest. Boys fought for the pride of being the Champion Shin Kicker. Winning the competition gave the winner the chance to brag about it for a whole year, when at the next fair he would be required to fight once again to keep the honour. I dawdled behind my friend, as we weaved our way through the thickly pressed crowds, I was constantly on the alert for Harriet's presence, but I hadn't seen her or her friends all day. Lucy Conway gave us an awkward but cheery wave as she caught sight of us, her arms loaded with purchases. As we neared the contest, a man walked by with his wife and tipped his hat towards Hannah. Turning quickly, I saw a crimson blush spreading over her cheeks as she smiled back, in acknowledgement. "Who was that ?" I asked accusingly, noticing that Hannah was trying to appear nonchalant, but I had known her too long and too well to be taken in by her lies. "Who was who ?" She asked, pretending innocence.

"You know very well who I mean. How do you know him ?"

"Oh that man, he knows my mother that is all." Narrowing my eyes, I tried to decide whether to believe her. "His wife didn't seem too happy that he seemed to know you." I chided, wanting to press her further.

"I expect she failed to recognise me is all, now come on are we going to watch the contest or not ?"

Bales of hay had been used to form a makeshift ring for the competition to take place. The noisy crowd cheered on the boys as they fought, their hair dripping in sweat as they grappled with one another making it difficult to hold onto one another. "What've we missed ?" Hannah asked one of the girls standing next to us who was busily admiring the masculine prowess on display. "You're just in time. Whoever wins this will be the champion." Privately, I thought that boys were indeed strange if they prided themselves on their ability to kick someone harder than anyone else, or take a kick to their ankles with more ability than anyone else. The eventual winner would act like a prince among men for a whole year and if past years were anything to go by, they would use their notoriety to woo a mate. They were no better than two stags, trying to outdo one another. Of the two boys, I recognised the dark haired boy from my visits to St Mary's Church. He was the eldest son of the Brading butcher and the local crowd were cheering him on. I winced as he lost his balance and fell over, followed by a loud groan and calls for him to get back on his feet. Inexplicably I found myself shouting for him finish the fight along with everyone else. The boy struggled to stand, but he was larger than his opponent and managed to push him over the line and win the competition to rapturous applause.

As soon as the winner had been carried out of the ring on the shoulders of his friends, the cockfighting began, with men betting in earnest on the outcome. Most of them were drunk and I guessed that most of them would be left with no money in their pockets and heads full of pounding hammers, whilst their wives berated them for their stupidity come the morning. I had no wish to watch the needless violence and the assembled men seemed more aggressive than before, so I allowed Hannah to pull me along towards the horse boat.

Chapter 5

Opening my eyes, I saw my father standing before me. He seemed to have aged in the few days since I'd last set eyes upon him, I forgot my feelings of remorse and focused on my concern for my father. "Are you well ?" I asked, trying to sound nonchalant. He smiled at me through reddened weary eyes. "Serving the Lord and tending to his flock can be quite tiring sometimes my dear. I stayed all night with Mrs Arnold, as she passed over into our heavenly father's care. She is at rest now thank the Lord, whereas I still have plenty of his work to do here."

"I see" I replied, reassured that there was nothing desperately wrong. I can only cope with one ailing parent at a time and my mother currently held that position. "I was wondering" I asked, fighting to keep the neediness from creeping into my voice, "whether you wanted to go for a walk with me ?" Some fresh air and a stroll with my father would clear my head and make me feel better. I yearned for my mind to be distracted from the crushing loss of William and the empty space he had left in the village and in my heart. It had been some time since I had spent quality time together with my father and I needed him now more than ever. I wanted to talk to him about William, so that it wouldn't come as such a surprise when a strange young man approached him, asking for his daughter's hand in marriage. "I'm sorry my dear" he replied, shaking his head regretfully, "I have to get home to Jane she's expecting me, maybe another time, but my new duties do keep me very busy at the moment."

In my heart, I longed for him to invite me back to his home to dine with him and his wife, but I knew that was something he would never offer, no matter how much I desired it. He wouldn't want to upset his wife at any cost. "I should be getting home now myself anyway. I need to go and check on mother." I muttered briskly, feeling my face redden in embarrassment. He winced, as I mentioned my mother and I felt a glimmer of satisfaction that I had managed to hurt him back, but then instantly felt ashamed of myself, for being so cruel to a man who always did his best not to hurt me. I was annoyed at myself for behaving like a spoilt child instead of an eighteen year old young woman. I walked away and realised with a sinking feeling that I had seen more of my father before he had come to work in Bembridge. He always seemed to be so busy now, though I suspected that it had more to do with his wife Jane and his own feelings of shame, than it had to do with needy parishioners.

No sooner had I stepped through the doorway of The Hatch, than I heard my mother calling out to me. The weight of guilt seemed heavier with each hurried step I took. Running to my mother's room, I cursed myself for spending so long away from home, it wasn't fair to keep neglecting my mother this way. "I'm here, I'm here. I'm sorry I'm so late." My mother had somehow managed to sit up by herself and her needlework lay unfinished in her hands. She seemed to have rallied since the previous day and I was comforted to see that she appeared to be recovering a little, at last. "Where on earth have you been ?" Were the first words that greeted me, before I even had the chance to say hello. Uncertainty flickered across my eyes, as I briefly wondered whether she had heard me leaving so early, but I decided that I would have been faced with more fury on my return, than a simple enquiry and sent up a silent prayer of thanks that I had not been found out. "I was unable to sleep so I got up early and went to the chapel to pray. I spent some time talking with my father." I felt grateful that I could look my mother in the eye and tell her at least a part of the truth, but I still felt uneasy, so I changed the subject instead. "Enough of what I've been up to. How are you feeling ? Can I get you something to eat ?" I asked, fussing with the blankets and the flowers by the window, anything rather than having to look directly at my mother. "I'd like some toast and some tea, then I think I shall come downstairs and maybe even do some work in the stillroom. I can't stay here in this bed, feeling sorry for myself, day after day can I ?" The colour had returned to her cheeks for the first time in days, but I was still uncertain whether her getting out of bed would be a good idea or not. One thing I did know all too well, was that when my mother had set her mind to do something, she would brook no arguments, so I smiled outwardly and hoped for the best. "I'll go and make that tea then" I said with a reassuring smile and went to carry out my mother's requests, hoping that everything would soon be back to normal, including William's return and his proposal of marriage. Keeping it a secret for several weeks was going to be difficult. There was still a tiny part of me that worried at his curtness on the beach and how he had been reluctant to hold my hand. I told myself he had merely been trying to distance himself, limiting the pain of our temporary separation. He had told me he loved me and I held onto that word, filtering out everything else, in an effort to keep sane whilst he was gone.

Over the next few days my mother recovered sufficiently and although she wasn't completely back to her previous best, she was able to sit in a chair working and gossiping as she had always done. Neighbours popped in to see her, asking for her advice or simply passing the time and all the while, she constantly gave me a stream of orders that needed carrying out. Two long weeks had passed since he had gone and there was still no news as to when he was likely to return. As the days passed, I found any excuse to be out of the house, hoping to pick up some gossip from amongst the villagers, when that approach failed, I volunteered to take William's aunt a tincture she'd requested for his grandmother who had taken to her bed, suffering with a relentless cough.

The day was dry and sunny, but particularly breezy as I approached the Gould's cottage near the shipyard where the gulls wheeled noisily overhead, waiting to dive on the shoals of fish brought in by the boats each day. Knocking on the door with a trembling hand, I tingled in anticipation of finding out good news, but worried whether his family already knew about our relationship and if they did. Did they approve ? No matter how much I loved their nephew, I was still an illegitimate girl with no money to bring to the happy alliance. I wasn't so blinded by love that I didn't realise I would hardly be his family's first choice for a niece in law, but I hoped they would see how much we meant to one another and I would be welcomed into the Gould family with open arms. "Come in" shouted William's aunt, as his three cousins in short trousers flew out of the door, nearly knocking me off my feet. Entering the house, I pasted on a smile and sought out Mrs Gould. "Hello young Molly, am I glad to see you. My mother is in great need of your excellent remedy, I swear it's the only thing to use against a stubborn cough." Blushing deeply, I regarded the other woman, with her ruddy cheeks and her sleeves rolled up to the elbows, her hands wet and red raw from washing clothes. From her welcome, I gathered it must be common knowledge that I was William's intended and the fact that his aunt seemed so happy about it, rather took me aback. I smiled as she came towards me, readying myself to be hugged tightly in congratulation and welcomed into the family, but instead she simply stood staring at me with her hands on her hips and a strange expression on her face. "Well…?" She asked, holding out her hand expectantly. For a moment I was thrown. I thought perhaps she wanted to be more formal and wished to shake my hand instead, but as I made to extend my hand, his aunt said "you did bring the tincture didn't you ?" I felt my cheeks turning bright red, burning as though they were on fire. I tried unsuccessfully to cover my confusion and embarrassment and produced the much needed tincture from my basket, where it lay alongside the other bottles and jars which I had yet to deliver to other customers. Mrs Gould seemed not to notice my discomfiture and handed over two shillings "thank your ma for me. I heard she is feeling better now, I hope she is fully recovered."

"Yes thank you, much better" I replied, glad to be on safer conversational ground at last. I decided that I needed to gather my courage and ask his aunt when William was returning, or else I would spend the rest of the day cursing myself for a wasted journey. "Have you heard when your William will be getting back from East Cowes, only I heard one of the villagers asking after him ?"

The sound of the boys playing outside could be plainly heard and the silence following my question. I was convinced that Mrs Gould could hear my heart, beating ferociously in my chest. William's mother had seen straight through my lie, her lips twitching at the corners, one eyebrow raised in mock surprise. "I believe they will be there for a few more weeks yet, so if you hear anyone else asking after him, you can let them know now can't you my dear. I wouldn't want to think of anyone sitting around wondering when William was likely to return." Feeling myself blush once more, I made my excuses, leaving as quickly as I could, nearly falling over a black cat sleeping near the doorstep.

Marching towards the home of my next delivery, I had no idea how such disappointment could be borne. Adding to my melancholy was the realisation that although Mrs Gould had realised I obviously had an interest in her nephew, William had clearly not mentioned anything about his own intentions towards me. Telling myself that he probably wanted to ask my father's permission before making his feelings known and hadn't had sufficient time before he disappeared to East Cowes, made the pain a little easier to accept. I determined that whilst he was gone, I would fill my time with prayers for his safe and speedy return and help my mother as much as possible, after all, once I was a married woman, I would have my own home and children to care for and my mother would have to manage without me running around after her and keeping the home and business going.

As the days passed, my feelings for William grew in intensity. I found I was almost in a state of constant fever for him. Each night as the sun began to set, I'd stand at the back of my house, rejoicing that another day had passed and that the morrow might bring William back to his home, back to me and our new life could finally begin.

On one such night, looking up at the fullness of the moon, I noticed that it was surrounded by a misty halo and I shuddered inwardly, it was a sure sign that a storm was coming. Over the years I couldn't help but notice that I aroused romantic feelings in others, toyed with them before rejecting them without a moments concern, but for the first time, I realised I was actually in love and just how much being in love could hurt and I felt real sorrow for the way I had treated other boys in the past.

One morning, as I returned home from church, I thought I saw William disappearing into the dim confines of the inn, 'great, now I'm seeing things and imagining him everywhere,' I thought to myself and carried on home to help my mother. Her health was much improved, but I still needed to tend the pigs, the chickens, the vegetable patch and purchase anything that we needed and there was always something extra that my mother needed doing. That evening, I sat sewing by the last rays of the sunlight slanting in through the window and as I briefly looked up, I thought I saw William, walking off in the distance, too far away for me to be certain. 'Lord save me. I think I must definitely be run mad with love' I thought wryly 'I hope he comes back to me soon.' My mother could tell something was amiss and I was grateful that she didn't pry, but I felt the need to talk to someone about my relationship with William Gould, or I worried that I would burst with the sheer pressure of keeping such a big secret to myself.

Chapter 6

Awaking with a start, I stared in indignation at the daylight waiting for me, just outside the window. I'd spent the night dreaming of my wedding to William. The bells pealing in celebration had seemed so real and I was irritated that my perfect dream had been curtailed too soon. I lay in my bed and tried to work out what could have rudely awoken me, when I heard the real chapel bells tolling a doleful sound. My heart leapt and a cold fear crept through my veins, chilling my whole body. Buttoning up my yellow blouse and donning a blue skirt I ran to find my mother. When I found her, she was already out of bed and dressed, her usually neat and tidy hair an unkempt mess, with strands of brown and grey floating around her face reminding me eerily of Medusa and her snakes. Looking out of the front window of the cottage, I saw our neighbours hurriedly making their way up towards the High Street. My mother ran out of The Hatch and I followed close behind. Across the way, we saw our neighbour Beatrice Woods the old woman who kept bees of which she was most proud. Beatrice was the eyes and ears of the village, with not much getting past her, as well as being a purveyor of the best honey anyone had ever tasted, or so she liked to boast. "Whatever's happening Beatrice ?" My mother called out to her.

"It's Thomas Bull and his brothers. They didn't come back in this morning and none of the other boats saw them. The men are forming a search party for them and the women are going to pray for their safe and speedy return."

Men hurried past without acknowledgment, running towards the haven and their womenfolk walked sombrely in file up towards where the new chapel lay. The children who were able to walk, grasped their mother's skirts, they knew something was dreadfully wrong but didn't know what and they were scared. I saw Helen Bull joining the line of women a little further in front. She clutched her new baby son tightly to her, as though she feared that she would lose him too. Agony was etched all over Helen's face and her eyes and nose were tinged with pink from crying. I was saddened to think that the last time I had set eyes upon the family, they had been celebrating the safe birth of their newborn son Thomas. I didn't know how I could ever bear to lose my William and I crossed myself for protection against such a terrible thought, I didn't want to waste any more time not being his wife. Life was too short and this current disaster was proof of that. My mother grabbed my arm for support as we walked together but I felt her starting to pull away from me as we reached the chapel door and I could feel her minimal energy reserves slowly beginning to wane. She didn't have to say it, I knew she didn't want to come face to face with my father after so many years apart, but she knew as well as I did that we would be the talk of the village if we had remained in hiding, rather than going to the chapel to offer support for Helen Bull and her three sisters in law. For his part, my father treated us as though we were perfect strangers. He led us all in prayer, his voice was raised in supplication, trying to drown out the sound of children shuffling and coughing and the four Bull women weeping loudly and praying with more fervour than ever before. Every single woman and girl in the church knew in our hearts that the same scene was played out far too often on the island and each fresh vigil opened old wounds, uniting the village in raw grief, from those whose loved ones were currently missing, to those who had previously lost their loved ones to the cruel unforgiving sea. The waters around our island gave the men a good livelihood, providing us with its generous bounty, but every so often, the sea demanded payment.

Despite the fact that none of us had eaten all morning, everyone remained, not wanting to be the first one to leave, the first one to look as though they didn't care for their community and the missing brothers. So we continued kneeling in the church, waiting for someone to bring us news.

Hours passed before it was agreed that the eldest of the village girls could take their younger siblings back to their homes, so that their mothers could pray without pausing to deal with their restless, hungry children. Praying as though my own life depended on it, I poured my whole soul into my pleas and opening my eyes, I saw Helen's distraught face. I couldn't believe that the benevolent God I had always believed in and loved, would abandon Thomas and Helen and allow such a good man to leave his wife and newborn baby son. How could his baby boy be left to grow up and not even remember his own father ? They had to be safe somewhere. I began to look around for my mother, in the throng of bent heads of women in supplication. My father knelt before the altar as he silently beseeched God to spare the lives of Thomas and his brothers, but my mother was nowhere to be seen. I suspected that she had hidden herself away. It had been the first time that she had lain eyes on my father in eighteen years and I knew how hard it had been for her to see him once again, under the scrutiny of so many of the village women. Tiptoeing quietly around the church, I made my way towards the door, trying not to disturb anyone. I reached the main door before I finally found her. She was sat with her back to the altar, hidden behind a pew, I was so silent, that she didn't hear me as I approached. Her shawl was wrapped tightly around her shoulders for warmth and as I crept closer, I saw that her runes were scattered across the floor. Her lips were moving silently and her eyes held the faraway look that only happened when she was in a deep trance. My mother had always been so careful never to be seen like this unless she had agreed to a private reading and in a place of worship the blasphemy was so much more blatant and my stomach churned in response to my panic. Slowly lowering myself onto a seat I looked frantically around me. The others were still surrounding the altar deep in prayer and I breathed a deep sigh of relief, that my mother's heresy hadn't been discovered. The witchcraft trials had been outlawed only a short time ago but the fear and the threat of being named as a witch was still a terrifying prospect.

The light was beginning to fade by the time that my mother slumped back against the chapel wall. I had already scooped up the runes, hiding them in my small drawstring purse before anyone else could discover them. My mother seemed confused as she anxiously scanned the floor, but I put one finger to my lip warning her to be silent. The heavy church door suddenly swung open and everyone turned in unison, holding our breath as we hoped for good news and an audible sigh went up as we saw it was only one of the village girls struggling to cope with her four younger siblings who had come to plead with her mother to return home. As everyone else returned back to their prayers, a young boy in tattered trousers that were much too short for him, crashed through the door at a run. "Quick... Come quick. The men have been found."

After hours of sitting still, there was an immediate rush for the door, with no room for politeness or etiquette. Neighbour elbowed neighbour in their haste to be outside, to find out whether it was good or bad news and I knew I would be nursing some bruises come the morning. The men who had previously been rushing in the direction of the haven, could be seen in groups walking slowly towards the Olde Village Inne where the candles burned brightly in the windows. "Are the men safe and well ?" My father called out to a group of them, as they passed. It was hard to tell whether the news was good or bad, as some of the men seemed to be in a jovial mood and others were more subdued and withdrawn. Everyone eyed Helen Bull and her sisters in law as we waited for the reply. "We had been sailing all around the place, practically went to France trying to find them, we had all just about given up hope of ever finding them again, when we turned back before it got too dark and there they were, right on the shoreline." At the good news, Helen Bull's knees gave way beneath her in shock and she buried her face in her hands, wailing afresh at how close she had come to losing her beloved husband. Her sisters in law helped her up, as they wiped their own eyes, crying tears of both relief and joy. The four women hurried away to their cottages to start tending for their loved ones who had been returned to them against all the odds. "Praise the good Lord above" said my father, crossing himself in thanks for their safe return. "I don't know if it has anything to do with the Lord, it was more like witchcraft if you ask me." Another man shouted, "those men just appeared out of the air like magic. No one knows how they could have got past us without being seen. All four Bull brothers swept overboard and all safe and accounted for, I have never seen the like."

"What about their boat ?" Asked my father, if the brothers were unable to fish, they, their wives and their children would be sent to live in the house of industry in Newport and nobody wanted to see that happen to four such well-loved families. "We found the boat further around the ledge near St Helens, not a scratch on her." We let the men continue on to the inn for a well-deserved ale, or three. My father returned to the chapel to give thanks and after saying goodnight to each other, we all hurried back to our homes exhausted yet ready to feed families and husbands and

97

gossip over the exciting events of the day. The whole village was in a buoyant mood. The brothers had been found safe and well and our prayers had not gone unanswered. Standing alone in the darkness, I turned to my mother, trying to make out her eyes. "What did you do ?" I whispered, fighting to keep my voice under control. "You've always told me not to do anything to cause witchcraft to be mentioned and there you are, reading your runes right there in the chapel." My mother furrowed her brow in annoyance. "I have absolutely no idea what you're talking about" she muttered and left me standing alone, watching her stalk off in the direction of the cottage. "Come along, you can't stay out here all night" she threw back over her shoulder, disappearing into the gloom.

By the time I crept through the door, my mother was nowhere to be seen 'probably in her room hiding from me' I thought and went to sit in the still room, trying to calm my temper. My hands trembled with hunger, tiredness and hunger, as I stood to reach for a small bottle of brandy, I accidentally knocked a wooden box onto the floor. The lid had fallen off in the fall and as I bent to pick it up, a small poppet fell out into my hand. The night had been warm, but suddenly I was chilled to the bone as I stared at the miniature effigy my mother had evidently hidden. The little figure was clearly meant to resemble Alys, the wife of Joe the blacksmith, but the figure's middle was stuffed as though it were pregnant, exactly as Alys herself was. I knew she had been visiting my mother, but I thought she had merely been seeking advice on how to conceive, my mother had obviously used a darker side of magic to aid with her fertility problems. With her carelessness in the chapel and now this, I felt distinctly uneasy.

Chapter 7

After a restless night with little sleep, I crawled out of bed and dressed particularly early. Leaving my mother a cup of tea beside the bed, I dug over our vegetable patch trying to work off some of my nervous energy, the vicious way I attacked the earth, set the chickens into a panic and the infuriated pigs snuffled out in the cool morning air to see what was happening. The few people around at this time of the morning, gave me a wide berth as I stormed through the village, my head hung low, trying to avoid all eye contact. My legs began to tire eventually and my stomach rumbled in protest, so I headed for home, feeling a little relieved that no one had made the sign of the evil eye against me. As I put my hand on the front door, the ducks on the pond just outside, quacked noisily, splashing in the sunshine, some of them making their way across the water in my direction, turning away in annoyance as I disappeared from view. Sunlight slanted in through the doorway, whilst the aroma of cloves and lavender, mingled with the dozens of herbs hanging from the overhead beams, though I failed to notice them any longer. By midday my mother would usually be busy in the stillroom making her herbal remedies, but today all was silent in our little cottage. Creeping carefully up the stairs I found my mother huddled in her small bed, covered in several blankets despite the warmth of the day. Overnight, her body had seemingly shrunk to half its size and her skin clung unhealthily to her bones. Her thin dark hair glistened with sweat, and her skin was a sallow shade of yellow and white, covered in the same slick sheen as her hair. "Mama, have you eaten anything ?" I asked brightly, trying to hide my dismay that she hadn't even touched her tea that I'd left her earlier. She simply swallowed, shaking her head. "I'm not hungry" she croaked. Her body might be failing, but her spirit was still mutinous underneath. I set about building up the fire, which had almost extinguished itself, trying to busy myself so that fear couldn't take a hold of me. I watched as the flames leapt higher, beginning to lick the wood satisfactorily, then set about warming the previous days stew. With some of the weak broth in a small wooden bowl, I approached the small figure in the bed. My mother tried to drift back off to sleep, the exertion of answering me, quite overwhelming her. The old woman didn't even have the will left to fight and meekly allowed me to prop her up, into a sitting position. I managed to get her to taste two spoonfuls before she pushed the bowl away with what little force that remained in her worn out, frail body. "No" she screamed, like a petulant child and the bowl and spoon clattered noisily onto the floor spilling broth everywhere. I helped my mother to lie back down and covered her in the blankets. Her body felt overly hot to the touch, but she shivered relentlessly, as though she lay in deep snow.

While she slept, I tidied around our few possessions, wiped down the ancient wooden table and laid out a clean tablecloth. I dusted the picture on the wall of Brading that my mother cherished and then swept the hearth until it gleamed like new. Once the fire had been rebuilt, I concentrated on making some of our more popular tinctures. There was always work to be done around the cottage and my mother had been so poorly of late, that I'd been able to escape my heartache of William leaving, by channelling my energies into hard work and worry for my mother's health. Herbal remedies were our main source of income, apart from the odd pennies that my father sometimes managed to spare now and again. I was always grateful for any help from my father, but my mother wasn't quite so happy. "He's living in a big house with that barren wife of his. He's got estates all over the place. He lavishes money on that nephew of his and yet we don't see any benefit from him. I never thought that he would be one to shirk his duty, not a man of the cloth." I always let her rage on unchallenged, even though it wounded me. I wanted to rail at her, that my father couldn't openly acknowledge me and that every time he gave us anything, his wife would take umbrage with him and make his life a misery for several weeks after and that he did as much as he was able. At least he had not totally abandoned us. I was simply pleased to be a part of his life, no matter how small and I knew that if he could, my father would give me everything. His wife Jane was still hopeful that she would successfully bear him a legitimate heir and jealously guarded every penny of my father's estates with a fervour that bordered on obsessive.

I found the afternoon to be quite therapeutic and was soon lost in my own thoughts while I boiled some chamomile and yarrow flowers to be made into a tincture to aid sleep, when the front door suddenly flew open, making me jump. "Come quick, my wife needs help. The baby is coming… now." Dropping a handful of sage, I turned to see Joseph the village blacksmith. I had known him all my life, his wife was expecting their third child and like everyone else in the village, the family always called on our services to assist with the births. Sweat poured from his face and I was certain that it wasn't just caused by the heat from his forge. Shaking my head in panic, I motioned to where my mother lay above, in her room. "My ma cannot help this time Joe, she's far too ill. You'll have to go and fetch old Sally from Brading." Joe clearly wasn't in any mood to travel further, when his wife was in so much pain and he grabbed my arm in frustration. Allowing me just enough time to unhitch the birthing bag from the stillroom, he took no notice whatsoever of my protestations that I wasn't the right person to help him. "I've never done this before Joe, I think you need someone with more experience." The blacksmith's grip was starting to pinch, but there was no malice in it, simply pure fear. "Everyone in this village knows you've helped your ma often enough times. If you don't help my Alys, then there's only me left, because this baby is in no mood to wait to be born." With a sigh, I entered the stifling little cottage that belonged to the smith and his wife, right next door to the noisy forge.

"Hello Alys" I said with an overly confident air. Alys' eyes were glazed over with pain and she lay on her back, unable to move. "Let us see how far along we are" I murmured, rubbing my hands in my mother's lavender and lemon concoction and trying to imitate her confident air. Joe left us alone and went to pace up and down in the forge out of the way of the business of childbirth and every so often, I would hear him shouting at his two children to remain quiet, though it wasn't long before they started to whoop and holler in excitement once more.

Gingerly I lifted her skirts and saw the top of the baby's head, the dark swirls of hair were wet with blood and birthing fluid. I swallowed hard, through the lump of panic lodging itself inside my throat. "Not long now Alys, the babe is nearly here." The pregnant woman groaned, giving a loud wounded cry. The head slowly emerged, but the nose and mouth were still dangerously covered. I praised God that the babe was facing the right way and wouldn't be coming out 'arse first,' as my mother liked to say. I'd never had to cut a mother before and I didn't want to have to try it for the first time, when I was alone without my mother's steady hand and common sense. "I need you to push one more time for me. Can you do that ?" Alys' reply was the cry of an animal in pain and I found myself wondering why a woman would put herself through such agony. Some water and blankets had been helpfully left for me and I prayed that I would have use of them very soon. Alys was far more robust than she appeared and within moments the sound of a baby's squall filled the room. Whilst her son screamed lustily at the rudeness of being thrust into the world, Alys pushed once more and the shoulders emerged, followed in a swift burst, by the rest of the body.

Gently cleaning the babe's nose and mouth and tenderly wrapped the bawling infant in one of the blankets and held out my arms out to Alys. "Congratulations Alys, you have a fine son, with a strong voice. You did so well, you barely needed my help" I smiled with relief. Once the afterbirth had been safely delivered and I was certain that the mother was relaxed and the baby was at suckle and so I crept softly out of the cottage. Emerging into the bright sunlight, I heard a loud clanging sound from the forge as Joe rushed towards me. "You have a fine baby, Joe. Both mother and baby are quite well, but I shall leave it to your wife to introduce you." A grin split his face from ear to ear and he hugged me, overcome by his happiness, pride and relief. "Thank you Mol. Wait there" he exclaimed over and over, disappearing into his home once more. Seconds later, he burst back outside, passing me a small purse filled with coins, before disappearing back inside once more to be with his wife and new baby son, as proud as though he were the first man in the world whose wife had ever given birth, even though this was his third time.

My feet were unsteady as I slowly weaved my way home, I had neglected to eat anything myself and though the birth had been relatively easy, I was physically, mentally and emotionally exhausted. My mother was still fast asleep and the fire still glowed when I returned, but I threw a couple of logs on for good measure. Finding myself some bread and a hunk of cheese, I forced myself to take small bites. With a couple of apples I'd found left over in the kitchen and some ale, I felt far more invigorated than I had in days and tried to remain positive. I attempted to make more salves but my hands shook mutinously each time I tried. When I'd assisted with the birth, I had instinctively known what to do and had been calm and confident, yet once it was all over, I thought of all the things that could have gone wrong. The baby could have been born breech, the child could have got stuck or the mother might not have been strong enough to endure the ordeal. My mother would have known how to deal with these things, but I was still relatively inexperienced and very glad that my first birthing had been an easy one, though whether Alys would have described it as 'easy' would remain to be seen. Making a mental note to check on Joe, his wife and the new baby the following morning and to take along a restorative draught for the new mother to replace her depleted energy, I took a large gulp of brandy. Giving birth may be dangerous in its own right, but there were many dangers that could still befall a young mother soon afterwards and I didn't want Alys brought to bed with childbed fever, when she had a husband, two daughters and a newly born baby son depending on her to take care of them. The shadows on the wall lengthened and my stomach started to rumble in protest. The stocks of remedies, salves and tinctures had been fully replenished and with the overly generous payment from Joe, it had been quite a profitable day. Heating up the rabbit and vegetable soup once more, I attempted to rouse my mother. I hoped to cheer her with the news of Joe and Alys' new baby son, as well as my own part in the happy event. "Come along mother, you can't sleep all day you know. You must at least try and eat something." There was no response and as I nudged her, I found to my horror that she felt unnaturally cold. All of the sunlight and warmth were sucked out of the cottage and an icy fist, gripped my heart. "Mother ?" Only silence met my reply. Pulling the blanket up over my mother's closed eyes, I drew the heavy drapes surrounding the bed and sat upon the floor, hugging my knees, weeping as I rocked backwards and forwards.

Darkness descended in the small room, but I continued my distressed lonely vigil, bemoaning the fact that William was still in East Cowes, when I needed him most of all. Morning came slowly, lagging behind the waning moon that seemed reluctant to relinquish its power to the rising sun. Wiping my eyes on the sleeve of my blouse, I grabbed a piece of stale bread, before making my way to the chapel. It was still very early and groups of men were already making their way to the fields, but no children loitered around outside and the women were yet to make their way to market, so I managed to pass through the village without being bothered by anyone.

Pushing open the heavy door, I entered the coolness of the church and sat down to await my father. With her head bowed, I prayed over and over again for my mother's soul. I had always firmly believed that if I followed the word of God, both in thought and deed, then I would be forgiven for being born illegitimate and would be able to enter the kingdom of heaven, despite my dubious parentage. My father had always told me that God looked after everyone in the churchyard, even those on the north side, where the criminals and outcasts were laid to rest. In her own quiet way, my mother had also been a God fearing woman, apart from the one time when she had conceived me and I fervently hoped that she had been forgiven for her transgressions and would be allowed eternal rest in God's holy kingdom.

The sun was at its highest point over the island when I finally heard the heavy door opening behind me and my father slowly walked up through the nave. He was hunched over as usual, far too weighed down with shame to stand properly. He saw me sitting in front of the altar and hurried to sit alongside me. "Are you quite alright Molly ?" He asked, concern etched all over his, already tired looking face. I tried to answer but the only sound coming out of my mouth, was a loud sobbing and sucking noise that was embarrassingly like a loud hiccup. My father put his arm around me, his act of kindness making me feel even more miserable. "It's mama" I whispered, once I had calmed myself enough to speak. "She died yesterday. I didn't know what to do. I didn't want to believe it. I sat next to her body all through the night, hoping that I was mistaken and she would awake…but she didn't…" Descending into sobs again, I fell against my father's wiry frame, as he sat in silence, simply holding me close to him, while I cried myself out. Once the storm had passed, I awkwardly excused myself and slipped outside of the door for a few minutes to get some air in my lungs. Ever since my mother had died, I'd felt like a crushing weight was upon my chest, stopping me from breathing properly. "I've taken care of everything, your mother will get a decent burial, have no fear. I know she always wanted to be laid to rest in Brading and I'll make sure that her wish is honoured." My father said, grabbing my shoulders in support. The tears still shone in my eyes, as I thanked him, for taking control when I needed him to. "What will you do ?" He asked uncomfortably, clearly afraid that I might ask to move into his home with himself and his wife. "I… I know not" I stumbled. "I suppose I will remain at the cottage and carry on our work as best as I can." He handed me a heavy purse, filled with coins, his expression sombre, the news had come as quite a shock to him and I could see the sorrow in his face. "You may need this to tide you over" he said, kissing me gently on the top of my head, leaving me to my prayers as other parishioners began to fill the church, claiming his attention, as they so often did.

Heading towards my empty home, there were more people passing through the village, going about their business. I kept my eyes cast resolutely downwards, hoping that no one would see fit to stop me and pass the time in idle chatter. Normally, I would be more than happy to be waylaid in conversation, but I wasn't yet ready for my mother to become the latest morsel of village gossip, for everyone to offer an opinion on. If I made it common knowledge, I would be forced to admit that it had really happened, that I had lost my mother. Pushing open the door, I had almost gained the safety of sanctuary within, when I heard my name being shouted in a high pitched shriek that could only come from one person. "I heard you've been asking after my William. You wouldn't wish to embarrass him, by being seen in public with someone like you. Would you Molly Downer ?"

Swinging my head around, I felt the first flames of fire begin to ignite within me since my mother had died. How dare Harriet Morey refer to William as 'hers.' The previous two days, I had only known fear and confusion, but now, I simply felt anger. Harriet's face was full of amusement, making me ball my fists at my side, "please leave me alone, I've just lost my mother." Harriet seemed a little less recalcitrant at the unexpected turn of events and I gave her no opportunity to speak, simply closing the door in her face as she stood staring at me with wide eyed shock

Chapter 8

My mother's body had already been removed for burial
and so I set about cleaning the cottage from top to bottom.
She had always kept things nice and clean and I was
determined not to be a disappointment to her memory.
Feeling numb with grief, I built the fire back up once more
until it roared and the sap in the new logs spat loudly
causing sparks, The Hatch always felt slightly cold inside,
even on the warmest of days and since I'd been left alone I
couldn't seem to stop the chill from seeping into my bones.
I cooked myself some gammon, potatoes and carrots,
falling upon the food as soon as it was ready to eat. Lack of
sleep had made me weary, so in desperation I drank a large
measure of brandy to fortify my nerves and fell into a deep,
much needed slumber. In my dream, I saw my mother once
more. I was crying because she had been refused entry into
heaven and her spirit pounded furiously on the door of the
cottage, demanding to gain admittance to her home.
Terrified, I suddenly sat upright with a jump, my heart
leaping in my chest when I realised that my dream had
crossed over into reality and someone or something was
thumping on the back door. I hoped that it was a neighbour
in need and not my mother's ghost waiting for me
downstairs. Outside, night time had already fallen, though I
was too befuddled by sleep to guess as to what the time
might be. I briefly toyed with the idea of hiding under a
blanket, but the banging was insistent, so with a trembling
hand, I went to find out who or what it was that wanted my
attention so badly. The stranger at the door was tall and
broad shouldered but little else could be gleaned, his hat
being pulled down low to keep his face obscured by

shadow. He might have looked menacing, but I was relieved to find that he was definitely a real person and not an angry displaced spirit. He pushed his way inside, staring wildly around the room. "Where is your ma ?" His voice was gruff and he seemed to be a man used to having his orders obeyed. I opened my mouth to make a reply, but it was still to raw for me to answer questions about my mother, so I fired a question back at him instead. "Who are you ?" The man didn't seem to be in any mood to answer me and paced warily around the cottage. "I said, where is your ma ?" He repeated, whilst I slumped onto a stool trying not to weep, there was no alternative, but to answer him, if I ever wanted him to leave me in peace. "My ma is dead, she passed away last night" I wondered why this stranger would be looking for a woman who had spent most of the last few years confined to her home with ill health. He didn't look like the sort of person she would have acquainted herself with if she could have helped it and I fought down my sense of rising panic. At my news, the man seemed to lose some of his brusqueness, lowering his voice and I noticed that his eyes were blue and grey and as turbulent as the sea. "Did she ever talk to you about the brandy ?" He whispered.

"No" I admitted uneasily, not wanting to know any more "what brandy ?" The stranger seemed to be out of his depth, both of us were clearly thrown by the turn of events and the recent revelations. I poured him some ale, watching whilst he drank it thirstily. "Your mother used to help us out with the brandy. She used to let us store it in the little building outside, next to the chicken coop. She was also very adept at keeping anyone from snooping around too." My head whirled with this new, unknown snippet of information about my mother. "Why would she do such a thing ?" I challenged him fiercely. I hated the fact that someone else, a complete stranger could know something

109

about her that I didn't and I felt unaccountably jealous. "Because we paid her mighty well for the risk. Seems like she was pretty good at it, if her daughter had no idea what she was about."

Frantically, I replayed in my mind, the times when my mother had avoided answering where certain monies had come from, or when she had prevented me from entering the little outhouse we used to keep the wooden logs dry on several occasions, claiming that there was a dog with a newborn litter of puppies inside needing to be left alone and other feeble excuses that I hadn't thought to challenge at the time. I had been brought up not to ask too many questions, about my mother's work and I had kept my own council as a form of protection for as long as I could remember. Questions were dangerous. Questions could get you and your loved ones hurt. "I'll be taking over the cottage and I'll also be glad to carry on my ma's work, helping you… for the right price, of course." My apparent turnabout was so sudden, that I saw the man's white teeth sparkling as he grinned at me from underneath his hat, his face still shadowed. "Very well miss" he said with amusement. "You'll get your first delivery, under cover of darkness tomorrow. You won't have to do anything, we'll store it safely out of sight. It's good French brandy. Once it's safe to do so, we'll come and collect it. You can expect to be paid handsomely for your trouble and I'll leave some brandy for your troubles." Shaking his hand, I found myself highly pleased with the unexpected bargain, I'd just made. "It's been a pleasure to do business with you, sir." Within seconds, the man had left and in the breeze that swirled in from outside, I felt the first stirrings of real hope. With the money that my father had given me, the money my mother had kept under her bed, the earnings for the brandy storage, as well as the remedies and salves that I made, I was satisfied that I should be able to live quite comfortably for a good few years. It made my heart sing, to know that my mother would be proud of me. In her own way, with little money to provide for the both of us, my mother had managed to keep a roof over our heads and equipped me with the means to make my own way in the world and now that such a tragedy had befallen us, I found that I was grateful to her, in a way I'd never realised when she was alive. Dropping to my knees, I thanked God for my good fortune feeling certain that he would not punish me for my involvement in what was obviously a smuggling operation, especially when I was only trying to make ends meet and feed myself. After all, it wasn't as if I were the one who was actually stealing the brandy.

Across the whole of the island, smugglers were considered to be heroes and those that tried to prevent them from carrying out their business, often came to an unhappy end. The revenue men themselves were often overworked and underpaid and highly susceptible to bribery. I was convinced that the visitor had been heaven sent, to help me fend off starvation and I was more than happy to assist him, with a completely clear conscience. My mother had always told me that God helps those who help themselves. The Hatch seemed so much quieter, now that I was completely alone and at night, every creek seemed magnified, in a way I had never noticed before. 'I think I shall have to get a cat' I thought to myself sadly. 'Either that, or have William come and live here.' This last option, made me laugh out loud into the silence, at my own daring. No longer having my mother to care for, to remind the village of my illegitimacy, left me free to marry without delay and a whole world that had once felt closed off from me, now opened up with exciting possibilities.

The following morning, I awoke at the crack of dawn, braving the cool air outside, intent on depriving the chickens of some of their warm brown eggs. Feeling invigorated after a good nights sleep, I devoured a hearty breakfast of eggs and thick white bread, slathered with a generous layer of golden butter, washed down with two cups of strong sweet tea. Dressing myself in my best, brightly coloured dress, the crimson and blue flashing pleasingly emphasising the contrast between my vivid gown and my pale creamy complexion, I tied my long blonde hair with a deep green ribbon, grabbed my matching hat with fresh flowers above the brim and set out for my father's chapel.

Walking through the High Street, I realised that news had spread quickly around the village and several people stopped me in my tracks, offering their condolences. Despite their good intentions, I still found their entreaties and enquiries painful, though I was heartened to see how well our neighbours had thought of my mother. Most of the women idly quizzed me over whether I would continue my mother's work of helping the community with their ailments, which seemed to be their main concern. I was suddenly hit with the realisation that I had inherited the sole responsibility for the smugglers and all the village's births and illnesses. Joe had obviously told them all how I'd helped Alys safely deliver his baby boy and two women who were showing signs of early pregnancy, asked how I was feeling, then without waiting to hear the answer, demanded to know if they could engage my services when their time came. Deftly evading their questions, I explained that I was still in mourning and would let them know, once I was out of my grieving period.

Passing the inn, I was relieved to see Hannah making her way towards me, wearing her favourite brown hat with her hair held in a tight bun at the nape of her neck and matching dress. "I'm so sorry to hear about your ma" she blurted out, enveloping me in a crushing hug, causing my lungs to burn in their need for air. "How are you coping ?

Why didn't you come and find me ? You look very well, I must say." Smiling, I assured her that there was no need for any concern. "My ma always told me not to be upset if anything happened to her and to make my own way in the world. Wallowing in self pity will not keep me from the poor house will it ?" Hannah squeezed my arm and we both shuddered at the thought. "I'm just on my way to pray for my mother. Would you like to come with me ?" Shaking her head, Hannah seemed to be on the verge of telling me something, but changed her mind at the very last moment. "May I call on you at home, later ?" She asked, "I have a secret and I will just burst if I don't tell someone about it."

"Of course," I said lowering my voice conspiratorially. "I may have some news of my own. I'll see you later. I want to hear all about it." We parted and I was so intrigued at what Hannah's news could be, that I almost tripped over two dogs fighting over a plump rat laying dead on the floor in front of me.

Inside the little chapel all was quiet and still, save for old Mrs Beech adorning the nave with bunches of spring flowers. Most people were busy about their business, getting the midday meal together and caring for their children or washing their clothes and gossiping in the sunshine. Taking advantage of the solitude, I prayed for several hours on my knees for my mother's soul and relaxed a little when I heard Mrs Beech closing the door behind her. When I felt assured that God would appreciate my devout pleas, I rose unsteadily on red and aching knees. Massaging my legs, I gathered up my little basket and headed back through the village. The sensation of a purse filled with heavy jangling coins was new and pleasing, against my leg, where it lay safely hidden beneath my skirts. Although I knew that I would have to be careful to eek out my money and make it go as far as possible, I found that I still couldn't resist the desire to spend a little of it. However, each time I tried to pay for items, I was thwarted in my endeavours. I tried to purchase a duck, a large block of cheese, a loaf of warm bread, a handful of ripe figs and a small bottle of ale, but each time that I tried to hand over any money, no one would accept payment. My mother had helped the entire village in her time and it seemed that everyone wanted to remember the debt they felt they owed her. I was grateful and touched by their kindness, so I thanked them and stowed the items safely in my basket, leaving my money to be spent another day. I had even picked up a particularly fine apple cake for when Hannah came to call upon me. I spent the rest of the afternoon, tidying the cottage, making my bed several times over until I was absolutely certain that the blankets had no creases in them and even managed to find the time to repair one of my own dresses, which would otherwise have been left for my mother to deal with. A couple of villagers suffering from an ague, had called at the cottage and paid me handsomely for a salve, so relieved were they that they didn't have to travel to the next village to get help.

I'd just started to doze in the sunshine when Hannah rapped on the door, pulling me out of my reverie. Ushering her in excitedly, I made her sit, untying my apron before finding two plates and cutting us each a slice of moist apple cake, dripping in its own syrupy sugar, glistening like a jewel in the sunlight. The last couple of days had been difficult, but I was in a mellow mood and focused all my attention on what my friend had to tell me, before I revealed my own exciting news. "Well I must say, you seem to be coping remarkably well." Hannah said with approval, looking around at the well-kept room, touching her bun at her neck in the way she always did when she was nervous and popped a large piece of cake into her mouth, groaning in pleasure and making me giggle, as I wiggled my toes pleasurably in the warmth of the fire. "My ma was ill for so long, I'm just relieved that she's not in pain anymore and I still have my father. I'll be fine, God will provide for me, in fact he has already." We sat companionably together in the warmth of the firelight, demolishing our two large slices of cake. "Actually, I have news to tell you." I put my empty plate aside, Hannah seemed to be growing fidgety with anxiety, but swallowing hard she replied "then you tell me your news and afterwards I'll tell you mine." I wiped the last of the crumbs from around my mouth before taking a deep breath. "I'm to be married to William Gould." Hannah choked on a mouthful of tea, her eyes opening wide in shock staring at me speechless. Hannah had often heard me talk of how I never wished to get married and as far as she knew, William and I had barely even spoken. "Goodness, congratulations" she spluttered, "when is the wedding to be ?"

"Oh we haven't discussed that yet." I sighed happily. "He's been working in East Cowes, but as soon as he returns home, he's going to seek out my father and ask him for my hand in marriage and then we'll tell everyone. We're in love, Hannah and I'm so very happy."

"You do mean the same William Gould ? The one that practically followed Harriet around like a dog outside of church that time ?" I bristled at the memory, angry that she should even dare to remind me of it, when I was trying to celebrate my life changing news with my best friend. "Yes, I believe we are talking of the same person and he did not follow her like a dog, he left to spare me any more lashings from her evil tongue. We're to be married and he's in love with me and that's all there is to it. Are you not happy for me ?" I stood with my hands firmly planted on my hips, tapping my foot, daring Hannah to answer with anything

115

other than a 'yes,' but my friend twisted her hands together, clearly uncomfortable. "I've just seen him going into the Olde Village Inne with Harriet's father, he's been around the village with her father for the last few days, but I haven't seen him with your father Molly." My legs buckled in shock and I sat myself quickly in a chair so that Hannah wouldn't notice, how much the news had affected me. "You must be mistaken." My words sounded hollow and I wasn't sure who I was trying to convince most, me or her. "No it was definitely him Molly. I would know him anywhere, he's been spending a lot of time in the company of old Mr Morey of late."

"But it can't be. Why would he have any business with Harriet's father and why would he not come and find me straight away ? He's still working in Cowes." I winced, as I heard the whining tone of my own voice. "That's something only he can answer I fear, Mol. I'm sorry, it seems you must seek him out and ask him. There will be a reasonable explanation, I'm sure." Hannah smiled meekly in an effort to clear the air. We had never had a disagreement before and I had no wish to have one on a day when we should be celebrating each other's happy news. I downed another brandy, feeling the need to explain my actions. "I've always held William Gould in the highest regard and if I'm to be bound to any man, then he's the only choice for me. I'm sure I haven't seen him yet, because he's working hard four our future, his dealings with Mr Morey will be about business."

"Well you know that Harriet won't like it at all, from what I hear, she's been hoping to catch his eye, herself, " muttered Hannah conspiratorially, causing me to smile with a hint of smugness. "I had never even thought of that" I replied sarcastically, "But now you mention it, I would consider it a very definite bonus."

Suddenly remembering that Hannah had some news of her own and relieved at a change of subject, I encouraged her to tell me. "Out with it Hannah. I know that you will be in a terrible mood if you don't confide in me this very moment."

"I've fallen in love too, my dear Molly" she gushed, "we've secretly been seeing one another and it's getting serious between us. We've been lovers for some time now." The gravity of her confession rocked me to my very core. I had no idea that my best friend had been entertaining boys and the thought that she might have given herself to a boy, before they were even wed was pure folly and a sin. I supposed that if Hannah and her beau were to be immediately betrothed, then any indiscretion could be smoothed over and her reputation might still be saved. The silence was palpable, as Hannah watched me, becoming more mutinous as the minutes passed. Grasping her hand, I tried to reassure her. "If you are happy my dearest friend, then I'm happy for you." With a sigh, her shoulders dropped and the tension left her body altogether. "He really is the most handsome man that I've ever met. I miss him so much when we're apart." I laughed at my friend's excitement. "Why have you kept him so secret for so long ?" I demanded, "especially from me." Uncomfortably, she anxiously twisted her hands. "He decided that we should keep it between ourselves, whilst we got to know one another better."

"Do I know him... oh is it young Jonathan the farm hand ?" Hannah wiggled uncomfortably on her seat. "No... I've never favoured Jonathan and well you know it." I thought for a little longer, but after naming all of the unmarried village lads, I was still no nearer to uncovering my friend's secret. "I'm in love with Colonel Malcolm Wheeler," she confessed at last and I reeled as though I had been physically struck. "There must be some mistake my dear, Colonel Wheeler is already married."

Hannah studied the floor, refusing to meet my gaze. "He's not in love with her, indeed she's an unwanted burden upon him. He assures me, that he's in love with me, in a way he's never before experienced." I gasped for air, desperately trying not to faint. My beloved friend, the one whom I told everything to, was no longer a good God fearing girl like myself, she was now delighting in sin and depravity. I had to try and save Hannah from her own selfish wants and from the clutches of the very devil himself. I'd known Colonel Malcolm Wheeler for as long as I'd lived in the village and it was well known that he had an eye for the ladies. His wife, was a figure of pity amongst the women folk, whilst the men always talked of her husband with a smile and a knowing wink. "You have to stop this terrible nonsense now, it's already gone too far. Surely you must realise there's no future for you both. He has a wife, that he was joined to by God himself and now you face eternal damnation for this great sin." Hannah's cheeks flamed deep crimson as she stood abruptly and marched out of the cottage. "I never want to see you again… You… you… sinner." I screamed, the tears finally spilling over my cheeks, as she fled from view. In the course of a few days, I'd lost my mother, the love of my life and then my best friend, just when I needed her the most. Wrapping a thick woollen shawl around my head and shoulders, protecting myself from the stiff cold breeze blowing straight across the island, I walked slowly towards my father's church. My heart was broken from all the pain of loss and betrayal and it was threatening to overwhelm me.

As usual, the cool confines of the church were a balm to my soul and I instinctively relaxed as I entered. Candles illuminated the altar, their flames flickering in the draught of the open door. I prayed for my mother as I had every day since her death, but for the first time, I prayed for someone else too, I prayed for the soul of my best friend. I was sure that Hannah had quite lost all of her senses and needed to be prevented from her course of action, before it was too late and all was lost. It was a sign of how cunning, Colonel Malcolm Wheeler was, that the whole village had been kept from learning of their secret. Usually in Bembridge, the whispers spread like fire through dried grass, but on this occasion, no one had been any the wiser. Just as the cold began to penetrate my bones, I noticed the flames flickering once more, signalling that my father had returned. I yearned to discuss Hannah's wanton behaviour with him, but how could I when he himself had succumbed to the sins of the flesh and fathered an illegitimate child, so instead, I merely mumbled. "I'm missing ma and I've had a falling out with Hannah. All will be well in the end though." Never one to linger when women were emotional, my father was satisfied that there was nothing more he could do and left me to my prayers. When I was emotionally depleted, I waved goodbye to him, left the church and secreted myself behind the thick trunk of a yew tree just outside the gates and waited.

Chapter 9

No one spotted me in my secluded place and for my part, I hardly dared to breathe as I kept my eyes firmly trained on the door of the Olde Village Inne. A cool breeze blew through Bembridge and I shifted my weight from time to time whenever I started to lose feeling in my legs, but otherwise I remained where I was, leaning against the rough tree bark, determined to find out if Hannah had spoken the truth. The shadows slowly lengthened and my heart leapt into my mouth each time the inn door opened. I was finally rewarded for my endurance, when I spotted William Gould emerging with none other than Harriet's father. Hannah might be immoral, but she'd told me the truth after all. William Gould had indeed returned home and if Hannah was right about everything, he'd been back in Bembridge for some time and he hadn't come to seek me out. My head spun in confusion. I knew that men liked to be the one in control in a relationship and they weren't encouraged by women who were too headstrong, but I'd never been the sort of girl to sit around and wait for anything to come to me. I needed to know what he was about, the matter wouldn't wait any longer and if he needed a little nudge to go and see my father, I would be pleased to provide it. Managing to stay at a discreet distance, I followed them until they stopped to shake hands and Morey went off in the direction of his home, whilst William unsteadily took the path leading down towards the haven.

Walking faster and faster, my heart hammering wildly, I finally caught up with him. My voice was too constricted by fear and excitement to call out to him and he hadn't heard me following him in his inebriated state. He wore a pale brown shirt with his sleeves rolled up above his elbows and dark brown trousers, held up by thick braces, his dark brown curls shone in the rays of the late evening sunset and my heart leapt in joy at the sight of him. He was even more strikingly handsome than I'd remembered and I was ecstatic, despite the gnawing terror in the pit of my stomach, that all wasn't as it should be between us. The new life I'd been dreaming of was in danger of being snatched away by the very man that I'd dreamed of having it with. I caught him by the arm, spinning him around to face me. Whilst I'd been waiting, I'd played out hundreds of possible conversations in my mind, yet when he was actually standing in front of me, I found much to my chagrin, that the only sound I could produce was simply, "William." He stared at me mutely and the hazel eyes that I had first fallen in love with, seemed vacant and glassy. "What do you want ?" He slurred and the stench of sour ale washed over me revoltingly. I'd expected to find him acting guilty, full of excuses for not coming to seek me out, but I hadn't expected him to be so truculent, acting as though he didn't even know me, his behaviour threw me. "I... I saw you coming out of the inn and thought I'd see if you were okay. You did say that you'd come and find me when you returned, I haven't seen you for weeks after all." Wishing that he would crush me to him in a welcoming embrace, I finished, shyly and almost pleadingly. "I've missed you." My words seemed to finally penetrate the drunken fug of his brain and his demeanour softened a little. "I've drunk overly much. I need to go and lie down I think."

"I thought that perhaps you might be on your way to see me." I said hopefully and as soon as the words had left my mouth, I wished that they hadn't sounded so needy and whining. My growing sense of unease doubled as he stood silently, staring at me as if I were nothing more than a stranger to him. "I couldn't" he finally replied, his face crumpling. "Forgive me Molly, but I couldn't, you must stay away from me." Considering the conversation to be at an end, William turned and continued walking home. Managing to stop in front of him, I blocked his path. "Whatever do you mean William Gould ? What's happened ? You said you loved me ? I thought that we were to be married." Tears of pity were threatening to spill out from the corners of my pink rimmed eyes, but I stood with my fists curled into balls, trembling. Engulfed as I was in anger and misery, I had nothing left to lose. "I got tired of waiting for you and your high minding principles, so I went and found a girl that wasn't so resisting of my charms," piercing my heart with every slurred word he uttered. He attempted to walk away once more and once again, I stopped him. Determined to make him change his mind, hoping that it was simply the drink talking, I stood in front of him one last time. The tears ran unchecked down my cheeks, falling in large splashes onto my pale green blouse. Our argument had drawn a crowd of onlookers, not much happened in the village and when someone was in such a state of hysteria and insults were being thrown around, it didn't take long for a sizeable group to assemble. William swayed uncertainly from side to side, whilst I furiously scanned the faces of those who'd gathered to witness one of the worst events in my life unfold, as though it were public entertainment and we were nothing but more than a pair of actors in a play. Part of me still expected William to explain that this was all just a cruel jape, before declaring his undying love for me, but I stared with dawning horror as Harriet Morey stepped forward out of the crowd, standing shoulder to shoulder with my William. "Just because you've lost your mother and your best friend left your house in tears earlier, don't make the mistake in thinking that you're going to steal my betrothed."

I stood rooted to the spot, I hadn't even flinched. I kept my eyes, firmly trained on William alone. "Your betrothed ?" I whispered, but he stared awkwardly at the ground and I despised him for the coward he was. Harriet was unhappy at being left out of the conversation, she wanted to ensure that she publicly humiliated me, as much as possible so, grabbing William's hand she forced me to look at her. "We were betrothed last week. The wedding's to take place next month. I can't wait to become William's wife, with both my mother and father proudly watching me." After years of altercations, Harriet still had the power to wound me. I hadn't even considered that when I eventually married, my mother would no longer be alive to witness the happiest day of my life and the realisation doubled my pain. "I'm sorry," was all he managed to mumble.

The gloating expression on Harriet's face was too much to bear and my fury made me careless. "May you never have a moment of joy and when good fortune smiles on you, may you never live to enjoy it Harriet Morey," I burst out. The change in the crowd was immediate. They'd been all too pleased to watch two young girls fighting over a handsome young man, but I had gone a step too far. I'd publicly cursed Harriet. A curse had not been openly heard in the village for many years and some of them were clearly afraid. Several people made the sign to protect them from the evil eye and I heard the word 'witch' being whispered. Whirling around in a panic, I felt a wave of horror crashing over me. I'd lashed out in my pain, but now the anger had subsided, I realised that I'd undone a lifetime of caution in one outburst. Gathering my skirts I ran full pelt, back to the safety of my cottage, where the onlookers and the dangerous word 'witch' were left far behind me.

Chapter 10

I took to my bed and didn't dare stir for two whole days. I
even missed my mother's burial, though there had been
several times when there had been a furious knocking at
the door and voices shouting to me that I wouldn't forgive
myself, if I didn't attend. On the fourth day, I heard
Hannah's timid tones beseeching me to let her in and my
fury blazed hot once more, making my blood boil and my
heart thump alarmingly. By the fifth day, the cheese and
figs had all been eaten and three empty brandy bottles lay
discarded upon the table, with the remains of their contents
leaking all across the table, staining the wood. My tongue
felt thick and furry and my head pounded unbearably,
making me see stars whenever I turned my head too
quickly. My hair which was usually shiny, hung dully over
my shoulders, sticking together in thick greasy clumps. My
mother had left me, my best friend was a wanton sinner
who was beyond all redemption, my father wasn't there for
me when I really needed him and William Gould, the love
of my life, had played me false in the worst way possible.
He'd allowed me to be humiliated and I'd allowed Harriet
Morey to get the better of me. The very thing that my
mother had told me to avoid, had come to pass. I'd always
thought that it would be a disgruntled or jealous customer
that caused problems, when in the end it had been my own
temper and Harriet's goading, for the village to point the
finger and name me as a witch. I didn't want to see anyone
else ever again, most likely they would only make the sign
against the evil eye if I did, or form an angry mob to force
me out of The Hatch and ultimately out of Bembridge

altogether and I resolved to remain in my own self-imposed fortress at least for the time being.

After several days, I decided that I should at least be safe to venture as far as the vegetable patch at the back of the house and collect some eggs from the chickens. Stepping gingerly outside of the door into a stiff Bembridge breeze, I found two books waiting for me in the small alcove in my wall, along with a loaf of bread, some cold duck legs wrapped in muslin and a small bottle of ale lying on top of an old stool that my mother had used whenever we had eggs to sell. Grabbing the items in confusion, I ran back into the house, slamming the door behind me. The fear that strangers had been just outside my door made me breathe heavily, and I tried to still the feelings of panic. Carelessly throwing the book of psalms on the table, I fell upon the duck ravenously, tearing huge chunks of bread in my hands and stuffing them in my mouth, until I couldn't face another bite. The cool ale slaked my thirst and it was only then, that I began to wonder about who had left me the food for my body and the spiritual books to nourish my soul.

Before the public cursing, I thought that it could be any one of a number of different people leaving goods out for me, but now everything had changed, I couldn't even name one person who might be trying to help me. Wrapping the remains of the duck and the bread into the muslin, I stopped up the bottle of ale, relieved that I could avoid people for at least another day. Idly picking up the first book, I found myself reading it from cover to cover, swiftly followed by the second one, though I was unsure if it was simply boredom that convinced me to read them as the words didn't have their usual soothing effect and I found that my lifelong faith was being severely tested, by my recent losses.

Awaking to a fine, bright morning, I dressed carefully in my best blue blouse with heavy puffed sleeves, full maroon skirt and a heavy brown shawl and ventured out of the cottage once more. My hand trembled on the door handle, as I prepared to face a village who now thought of me as a witch. Yet again there were books left in the wall cavity and a bag of provisions on the old stool, in addition there were also two small purses hidden behind the books. I was thankful that I could remain in my own company for at least one more day and exchanging the new books for the ones I had already read, I hurriedly grabbed the bag of food and drink and the purses, slipping back inside before anyone saw me. Storing the provisions carefully away, I opened the smallest of the two drawstring purses. Inside the first, I found a shilling and a small crude drawing that looked similar to the bottle my mother always used for her cough remedy. The second purse contained a handful of half-crowns, which was likely my payment for turning a blind eye to illicit brandy on my property. Stowing the coins behind a loose brick next to the fireplace, I selected a bottle of cough remedy and placed it back outside on top of the stool, hoping that whoever who had gone to such pains to let me know they needed help, would return to see if their request had been answered. With no desire or reason to venture into Bembridge, I settled down to some sewing, relieved at the peace. I hadn't touched the besom for days, but I no longer cared, I was the only one who would see it after all and my mother was no longer there to chide me, what did it matter if everything became coated in dust ?

The daylight streaming in from outside began to dwindle, so I placed my needlework to one side and stoked the fire before it burnt out altogether. Just outside the door, birds twittered cheerily and I felt an overwhelming need for some fresh air. Finishing my meagre meal of fish and the green beans that represented the last of my provisions, I left the dirty plate to be washed up later in the evening, fastened my hat and drew my brown shawl tightly around my shoulders, quietly leaving the cottage by the back door. Night time descended quickly, chasing the sun from the sky as I skirted around the west of Steyne's Copse, past Mellons and headed in the direction of Knowles' Farm and my favourite sanctuary. The closer I got to the windmill, the grass lengthened and I felt the pull on my muscles as I ascended the hill. Inside the mill was dark and silent and the towering sails were still, although they creaked from time to time in the breeze. There were many in the village who thought this an eerie place to be alone at night time, but I revelled in the solitude. Whenever I had a dilemma to mull over, I found this a good place to just sit, hugging my knees until I felt the calmness creeping over me and I could breathe easily once more. But I hadn't been here since the fateful day that William Gould had pounced upon me and the memory of happier times made the tears fall, unbidden. Looking up at the blanket of stars shining in the inky blackness high above me, I wondered whether my mother was up there in heaven watching over me. "I know that you would not have approved of my outburst at Harriet Morey, but it was not my fault. She was the one who provoked me. She stole the love of my life and thought to mock me for it and you should still be here with me to help me through this." I shouted angrily into the darkness, but although I listened intently, the only response was an owl flying out of the trees to my right, making me jump. If William and Harriet were really betrothed, there would be a wedding in the village, a cause for much celebrating, feasting and drinking and it would be the main topic of conversation for months to come, unless another wedding followed swiftly behind. I resolved to shut myself away until the unhappy event was all over, even if I could withstand the gossip, there were the hostile villagers who thought of me as a witch, Hannah revelling in her secret sin and then there was William, joined to my very own mortal enemy just because I hadn't allowed him to have his way, it was too much to be borne. I was completely unrepentant, about the curse I'd placed on Harriet, in fact, every time I thought of it, my hope that it would become true, strengthened.

A rabbit hopped up out of the ground next to where I sat, taking one look at me, it promptly popped back into the safety of its hole once more. Immediately after, a large buzzard swooped down beside me, hitting the ground with a heavy thud, expecting to find its prey but it seemed to become nervous as it sensed me silently regarding it. Slowly it turned and flew away, thinking better of chasing after the rabbit, lest it become prey itself.

Fingers of icy coldness crept slowly over me, seeping into my bones, the bonnet and shawl were not enough to prevent the pervading bitterness any longer, so I returned to the warmth and seclusion of my own home, just as the cautious rabbit had. Entering the dark cottage, I lit a solitary candle and made my way straight to my bedroom, lying under the heavy blankets trying to conserve some heat. Scenes from the day, swept through my mind and just as I was just about to fall into a deep slumber, I found myself shocked into wakefulness by a loud pounding at the door. "Molly, Molly are you in there ?" I failed to recognise the gruff voice, but I could easily identify the panicked tone of, either someone whose wife had just gone into labour, or the helpless father of a sick child. I was only halfway to the door when I heard the man shout, "the babe is teething and my wife's beside herself. Please help us." The desire to run back to my bed and hide was overwhelming, but I wouldn't be able to bear the guilt of knowing that I could prevent a child's suffering and yet do nothing, I sighed at the weight of my responsibility for a village that despised me. "Put the coins on the stool at the back of the cottage, leave for five minutes and I'll leave you some tooth rub," I shouted through the heavy door. I could tell the man was a little startled, by the faint strangled sound of agreement he made, yet thankfully he did as he was asked without argument. Once I was satisfied that he had left, I slipped out under the cover of darkness, quickly palmed the shilling and left a jar of rub for the baby's inflamed gums. It was a relief not to have to deal with other people, but it was comforting to know that at least some of the villagers still had a use for my services and I could continue to afford food for the table.

Whoever was still leaving me provisions each day could probably ill afford to keep supplying me with goods, so after the frantic father had disappeared with the baby's rub, I left a note weighted down by a handful of pennies and asked for the money to be used to purchase the items on the list that I needed. If my plan worked, it meant that there would be no need for me to ever leave The Hatch, unless I decided to. I also, left the two religious books that had miraculously appeared in the wall earlier this morning and had kept me entertained for a very pleasant afternoon. With each new day, I expected to feel the desire to mix with other people once again, yet every day I found the fire of fury burning as brightly as ever and so I remained indoors hidden from view, except for my nightly excursions up to the windmill under the reassuring cover of darkness with only the wildlife for company. The mysterious kindly neighbour had taken my money and the list I'd left and purchased everything I required, leaving me pleased with this satisfactory arrangement. Word had clearly gotten around that I would not admit anyone into my cottage and so whenever villagers needed my aid, they would either bellow through the door, or place a note underneath and a few pennies on the wall outside, which I then exchanged for whatever they required and I found that I was amassing an impressive amount of money, which was safely stowed with the rest of my wealth, behind the loose brick near the chimney.

Chopping firewood one morning, I thought I'd heard Harriet's high pitched tinkling laugh, before I realised I was mistaken, the impulse to run and attack her with my axe, chop her into small pieces and hand feed her to the pigs, was almost too much to resist. Taking deep calming breaths, I tried to relax and stilling my violent urges, I repeated the words I had uttered on that fateful day in the village, the day that had marked me out in everyone's minds, as a witch. Time had only served to make the wish more potent and I felt a gleam of satisfaction, as I whispered, "you are going to get what is coming to you Harriet Morey. I'll make sure of that if it's the last thing I do."

Chapter 11

Creeping back from one of my nightly sojourns to the windmill, I was surprised and more than a little annoyed to find Hannah standing at my back door, trying her best to peer through the windows. "Oh" she exclaimed, jumping back in shock. "I thought perhaps you were ignoring me." Nudging her roughly out of the way, I made to walk past her and into my home without a word, but Hannah was evidently not in any mood to be ignored. "I came to warn you about Harriet. The whole village is buzzing with the news, they're like an angry swarm of bees." I was just about to slam the door, but her words penetrated through my heavy cloak of anger. "What ?" I asked tersely, despising myself for being so feeble. "Well you know how you said, that if she had any good fortune, she would never live to enjoy it?" Icy fingers of foreboding crept stealthily up my spine and my mouth suddenly felt very dry. I couldn't speak, so I merely nodded, indicating for her to go on even though I wanted to stop up my ears and run away and I loathed Hannah for managing to catch me out. "The wedding was supposed to happen next week and as a present, Harriet's aunt in Freshwater sent her a large sum of money." Hannah was obviously uncomfortable discussing Harriet and William's betrothal with me, but I let her continue uninterrupted, biting my lip and hoping she would be finished with the torture soon. "At the very same time that the money arrived, Harriet was out shopping and witnesses say she was suddenly stricken with a seizure, as she stood in line waiting to buy some fish. Joe and a couple of the other men carried her home and ever since, she's been unable to talk or move by herself. Everybody is saying it's proof that the curse is working and that the calamity is all your doing." Unable to stand it any longer, I slammed the door in her face, falling onto the seat nearest the front window, trembling, my blood was singing in my veins, I'd never felt so excited and empowered in my life. Only hours before, I'd repeated my curse, with even more enthusiasm than the first time. I'd sworn that Harriet would have her comeuppance and immediately after she'd received good news, the power behind the curse had been borne out. Elated, I felt fully alive for the first time in months and for once I managed to sleep soundly in my bed.

In Bembridge and across the whole island, the seasons slowly changed one into another, yet inside The Hatch everything carried on in much the same way that it had before. New books were still being left on a regular basis and so were the provisions. The angry mob had thankfully not turned up at the house ready to force me out of the village, but every now and again an overly confident child who wanted to show off in front of their friends, would throw some dirt at the windows and shout "witch" through my door. One morning I even woke up to find the words 'Witches Hatch' daubed across my window at the front of the house. William had destroyed my faith in men horribly, but now that the word 'witch' was attached to me it was clearer than ever that I was destined to be alone. Much to my dismay, even my own father had not visited to check how I was, he'd abandoned me too, probably too ashamed of my actions to want anything more to do with me. I would never have a husband, never have children and thought the thought chilled me, the realisation that now Harriet would never have those things either, lightened my spirits considerably and I chuckled to myself in delight. The cottage was covered in several inches of dust, blackened with age and the residue of countless wood fires, yet I no longer cared. Cobwebs had started to make their way into every corner and were slowly marching their way across the ceilings. 'May as well make the house, look like a witch's house, give them all what they want,' I thought, staring listlessly at the flames leaping higher in the fireplace.

When I was a young girl, my mother would sit beside this very same fire, regaling me with tales of women who had used their healing powers and knowledge of remedies for ill. Being a devout Christian, I'd relished hearing about curses, hexes and spells, as any other little girl who likes to hear a scary story in the safety of her home, near the fireside. Now as a grown woman, I thought of those tales, trying hard to recall them and wondered whether I myself had suddenly become the subject of stories to frighten young impressionable girls into being respectable. They had brought me to this predicament, every one of them. My parents had abandoned me, my best friend had let me down, and William had cast me aside, stealing my dreams from me. Harriet was clearly the most to blame, she had brought this on herself, with her gloating and her superiority. She'd mercilessly tormented me since we were children and now she was paying for it and that could only be considered as divine justice. The rain lashed angrily against the cottage making the candles gutter wildly in their holders. Seated in front of the fireplace, I held up the two miniature figures, admiring my handiwork. I'd created them from two small pieces of wood and dressed them in little clothes I'd fashioned out of rags and sewn carefully together. The one resembling a female had long brown hair, whilst the male possessed short dark curls. Their surfaces shone in the leaping candlelight, making them look as though they were truly alive and I prided myself on the fact that anyone looking at them would know in an instant that they were perfect representations of Harriet Morey and William Gould. Once I was satisfied, I marvelled at their perfection. "May you never be together in life. May you never recover from this affliction." I laughed, regarding the female poppet. "I bind this curse to you both." I said the words, as I wrapped a small black ribbon firmly around their bodies, fastening it with a pin, before hiding them high up inside the chimney breast next to the others. I didn't want anyone else to know what I'd done, didn't want to confirm their allegations against me and I was secure in the knowledge that no one would find the figures in their hiding place, but knowing that I had made them, gave me strength over my enemies. Satisfied, I laid the logs back in the fireplace and stoked up the fire, before wiggling my toes against the luxuriant heat, falling into a long, deep slumber.

The requests for help still came, though they were slightly less frequent than they had been and my visits to the windmill were far less frequent too. I began to revel in my notoriety, which was proving quite effective at keeping everyone at bay. I found it quite liberating to have nothing left to fear, nobody left to lose. I had long since made peace with the realisation that I would never be married. Until I had met William Gould I had been determined never to be joined in holy matrimony with anyone and now that I knew that he would be paid back in full and equal measure for breaking my heart, I found it easier to finally accept my situation in life. If the alternative was to chain myself to a fickle liar, then being alone was a far more agreeable prospect.

Chapter 12

The winter nights had begun to draw in once more and forced to abandon my sewing due to the failing light, I sat peacefully, munching on a steak pie that had been left for me earlier. The evenings being much longer, I found that apart from making more remedies, tinctures and salves, I actually did enjoy reading the religious texts, they were becoming a comforting way to pass the time. I missed the soothing influence of the chapel and the books were the next best thing. So much time alone, left me time to dwell on everything that had gone wrong in my life. I was exhausted by my own company, no longer able to bear being estranged from my father. I was well aware that he was probably ashamed of me, but I was still his daughter and after all, he was a man of God. He would have to forgive me eventually, no matter how upset he was. Deciding to go to the chapel and seek him out, I reasoned that if we were face to face, he couldn't ignore me any longer. My hands trembled erratically on the clasp of my cape, but I was determined to end the silence between us for once and for all.

With the shadow of night creeping across the sky ever earlier each evening, I often slipped out unnoticed with a shawl pulled up over my long blonde hair, evading detection, wandering around the chapel. I no longer entered the building, preferring to remain unseen in the darkest corners of the cemetery, yet still deriving great pleasure from being so near the house of God, a place I associated so closely with my beloved father. With so much time for reflection, I'd long since stopped blaming my mother for leaving me, I'd even managed to grieve for her and to my surprise I found that it had given my soul, a much needed release.

As soon as I reached the chapel. I felt my father's personality radiating out of every piece of stone. After spending countless days and nights seated alone in front of the fire, the early winter wind made me shudder, whipping my shawl around, threatening to expose my identity and I felt a strong yearning to return to the safety and solitude of my own hearth. Standing outside the large heavy door, I desperately tried to sum up the courage to enter for the first time in many months, but before I could, a man came flying out of the chapel door towards me. Surprise rooted me to the spot and I was relieved to see that he was a stranger, someone who wouldn't recognise me and raise a hue and cry. Yet, I felt somehow saddened that I hadn't played a part in Bembridge life for so long, that there must be whole families I would no longer be aware of. He was in such a hurry that he almost walked straight into me, failing to see me under the cover of darkness. I was dressed from head to foot in black clothing and obscured by the leafy branches of the trees, used to melting into the background, unseen. "I'm very sorry miss" he apologised, clearly flustered and lost in his own thoughts. "It is no matter" I smiled, pleased to be talking to the one person in the whole of Bembridge, who wouldn't point me out as the village witch. "Is anything wrong sir ? Can I be of any assistance ?" It has long been a habit of mine to always be on the alert for customers that may have need of my potions and this man seemed to be in some distress. Dabbing at his eyes with a white handkerchief, he cleared his throat noisily. "No my dear, though it is kind of you to ask" he shook his head sadly, "I'm afraid that I'm to be the bearer of bad tidings to the village. I've just heard that our good reverend, Jonathan Barwis has passed away. The poor man's been confined to his bed for the last few months and lacked the strength to fight any longer. I'm sorry, I must be away, but if you feel that you would like to come and talk or pray, I shall be in the chapel all day tomorrow saying prayers for Reverend Barwis' soul." Speechless, I watched as the man stalked off speedily towards the inn with his important news, little knowing what a terrible shock he'd just delivered. I ran for home as fast as I could. My throat was raw as I went, my shawl fell away and my hair streamed along behind me, but for once I didn't care who saw. As soon as I gained the inside of my home, I slid down the length of the door and finally collapsed, sobbing hot wet tears, that ran down my face, splashing all over my black skirt. Once again, a loved one had left me. I was now an orphan and I'd never felt so alone.

*   *   *

The slow, insistent rising of the pink and orange sun brought me no relief from my pain. I fumbled inside the chimney breast, pulling out the two poppets, I'd stored so long ago. They were blackened from smoke, but not enough to hide any resemblance to William Gould and Harriet Morey. Tightening the ribbon that still remained wound around them, I repeated the curse again, yet this time with more anger and placed them back out of sight, in their hiding place, inside the chimney. I had no appetite, but my stomach grumbled treacherously, so I slipped outside to see if the chickens had laid some eggs for my breakfast. A dewy mist crept along the ground and although it was still early, I found a note left for me on the rickety weather-beaten stool. Thinking that it would be another request for a simple love potion or a wart remedy, I was shocked to read 'Molly, I am sorry to tell you that your father has passed away. If you will not come to the chapel to see me, then I shall call back on you later this evening. I

137

would really like to talk to you' it was signed 'Reverend Henry Thompson.' I felt the ground tilting as I began to sway perilously from side to side. Gripping the stool in front of me, taking several large gulps of invigorating morning air, restored my senses, though I had quite forgotten all about the eggs. Tossing the note from Henry Thompson into the fire, I watched until every piece had been devoured by the flames. It felt too soon for my father to be replaced, though I had no doubt that it was just what he would have wanted, but overwhelming grief prevented me from being rational. Each time there was a knocking on the door, I ignored it. 'He'll give up before I do' I thought, carrying on about my business once I was certain that Henry Thompson had left.

One morning I found a purse left outside for me. Curiously I opened it with trembling fingers and inside found a handful of pennies and one of my father's bibles. He had been a wealthy man and I knew that he would have wished for his only daughter to benefit from his many estates, but his wife had obviously seen fit to exclude me and there was nothing I could do, except hold on to the fond memories of my beloved father. Throwing the purse and the bible against the wall, I paced wildly around the room, wondering how to exact revenge on my stepmother. Staring into the fire, I drank one brandy after another. When in a temper, I could match any man in the Olde Village Inne for holding my ale and I managed to sink a few bottles before my vision began to blur. Just as I was in danger of falling asleep, a thought popped unbidden into my mind. Fetching a piece of wood from the logs neatly stacked next to the fireplace, I began to whittle a female figure. Using some material from my sewing bag, I deftly sewed them into the rough shape of a dress, adorning the wooden poppet with its tiny clothes. The likeness to Jane Barwis was unmistakable and eerily similar. Dowsing the miniature figure in water, I said firmly, "may money flow as water through your hands. May it ever float away from you and never be in your possession. This is my wish." Pushing the poppet inside the chimney breast alongside the others, hiccupping softly, I made my way slowly and unsteadily to bed, safe in the knowledge that Jane Barwis had been taken care of. As I fell into a satisfied sleep, the ghost of a smile played across my lips.

*　　　*　　　*

It was a long time before I felt strong enough to venture out at night again, but the lure of fresh air was strong within me. I found it quite liberating to remain hidden, yet still feel a part of the village at the same time. I watched the odd person straying out after dark and wondered what business took them away from their hearths on such a bitterly cold evening. On one such evening, from the darkness of the chapel cemetery I spotted Hannah and Colonel Wheeler. The couple walked slowly towards the harbour together, making my hands clench in fury. The loss of our friendship had evidently meant nothing to my erstwhile friend and despite my opinion on the matter, she had continued with her doomed relationship. I wondered how long it would be, before the Colonel lost interest in his new paramour, casting her aside for a more interesting proposition, then where would Hannah be ?

Later, as I sat in front of the fire staring at the little poppet I had just made, which bore an identical resemblance to Hannah, it was an extremely good likeness and I prided myself on my talent for making them. The figure was identical in every way, except for the fact that this version, had a large bump under her miniature smock dress. "May your shame and your misdeeds be clear for everyone to see and may you be left alone to carry your burden." Hiding the figure along with my mounting collection of people who had wronged me, I looked down at the blackened smoke residue on my fingers and smiled, now everyone would know of Hannah's secret life of sin.

Chapter 13

Winter had the island firmly in its grasp, people tended not to venture out of their homes so much after dark if they could help it, at this time of year and the nights seemed endless, for those of us left alone with only their own company to pass the hours.

One evening, eating a bowl of stew, I heard someone moving around at the rear of the house. Flying across the room, I threw open the door, fully expecting to find a note from a young girl in trouble, or someone in need of a love potion or some other necessity that would bring them to my back door so late in the evening. The light from the cottage illuminated the small dark garden just enough for me to make out the faceless smuggler who'd visited me so soon after my mother's death. He still wore the same dark hat as before, still reluctant to be seen even though we were now partners of sorts. Leaning forward he placed a purse of money into my outstretched palm. "Your cut" he said gruffly and I threw the purse into the empty space behind me as though it were of no consequence. He didn't usually call on me in person, the money was normally left in the garden and for whatever reason he'd seen fit to visit me, I decided to take full advantage of the situation. "I want you to take me with you, next time." The steely resolve in my voice, echoed through the fields beyond. The surprise of my request, making him flinch. "Where ?" He asked incredulous, moving imperceptibly away from me, as though he would escape if he could, but something about my gaze, seemed to hold him fixed in place. "Take me to collect the next shipment of brandy with you ?" He snorted derisively, no longer in awe of me. "This is no leisurely day trip to the beach, you know. This is a serious business. People get killed running goods across the channel." I sighed ostentatiously as though he were boring me. "I know full well how serious it is. I was thinking that you would be least likely to arouse suspicion if you appeared to be a gentleman out with his girl for the evening." He stopped to consider my words and I knew that I'd successfully argued my case. "You might be onto something there. Very well, I shall send you word of when the next shipment is due in." Watching as he disappeared from view, I felt a frisson of excitement running through me, at the new direction my life had suddenly taken. If I was going to take the risk of storing the brandy, I reasoned that I may as well enjoy the thrill of collecting and delivering the illicit goods, into the bargain. My new found status as the village witch and a recluse, would ensure that no one would suspected me of being involved in such an operation and I felt protected and reckless at the same time. Each night, I paced the cottage, waiting for a sign and as each night merged into morning, I wondered whether the stranger would keep his word after all. When the sun made its first appearance in the early hours of every morning, I would creep out to the outhouse, but it was always empty, covered in dirt and cobwebs, closely resembling the interior of The Hatch.

Stepping back inside after replacing the latest books, I wondered whether I should perhaps clean the cottage, but the thought of all the work it would involve and all the energy I'd have to expend, made me sigh in despair, so instead I decided to simply ignore the detritus building up around me. The previous night, I'd heard a scratching sound, followed by a scuttling, but I didn't investigate too far, lest I be faced with an infestation of vermin running around the cottage foraging for food and wondered briefly, whether I should put a kitten onto my list of requirements.

So far I still didn't know who bought my daily shopping for me and the religions books. In truth, I was not overly curious. I thought perhaps it was best that I didn't know, for if I did, there was the chance that I may start talking to them and if we had an argument, I would lose the one last person on the whole earth who cared for me.

The following morning, just as the first of the suns rays began stretching themselves across the heavens, I went to find myself something to eat and noticed that someone had pushed a scrap of paper underneath the back door. Grabbing the note, I threw a couple of heavy logs onto the fire, the morning was still cool and I moved nearer to the window, where the light was far better to read by. In a heavy, shaky hand, were the words 'Tonight. Be ready.' A delicious shiver of anticipation ran all the way up my spine and the small fine hairs on the nape of my neck, stood stiffly to attention. This was what I'd been waiting for, these were my kind of people. The ones on the periphery of society, the outlaws and I would be going on an adventure with them. As my evening was to be spent, dealing in cheating and thieving. My excitement meant I could eat little, though I drank a few cups of brandy for courage, stiffening my resolve. I seated myself next to the window, tracking the slow journey of the sun through the heavens, excitedly waiting for night time to fall. Outside, I heard the chatter of women as they passed with baskets on their arms and the high pitched laughter of children scampering over one another in excited play. The cottage had begun to make me feel claustrophobic, I'd spent so many hours confined within its walls and with every passing day, it seemed more and more impossible to be outside and other's happiness only served to make me feel more bitter. At midday, I looked carelessly out of the window and spied Hannah walking on the other side of the road, trying for all the world to act nonchalant, with her downcast eyes, but nevertheless I could see that they kept sliding towards The Hatch. It wasn't easy to tell, because of the cut of her clothes, but I fancied that my nemesis was looking decidedly thicker around the waist than she had before. Raising a cup of brandy in the air, I silently toasted her. "To the health of you and your baby" I shouted, dissolving into gales of laughter, all alone in my silent little cottage.

Darkness fell across the island, as I sat rigidly waiting for my stranger to come and whisk me away. Uppermost in my mind, was how I could find out for certain whether Hannah was indeed with child, when I heard a soft rapping at the back door. Sweeping up my darkest shawl and hat, I covered the space between me and the door in the same amount of time that it took to take a breath and I found myself face to face with the gruff voiced man. I wondered where he came from, I didn't recognise his voice, but I knew that I'd been alone for so long, that I didn't even know my own customers any longer. "Are you ready for this ? You're not going to whine if it becomes dangerous are you ?" He asked and I snorted, bristling at the insult. "You'll be the one to whine before I do, I'll wager" I answered with a confident smile, hugging the shawl closer to my body, as the wind whipped around the walls of the cottage. "We need to go" he growled and resolutely closing the door on my only safety and sanctuary, I followed the stranger out into the unknown. The stars gave the only illumination in the sky, the moon being at its darkest point, the best time for carrying out our clandestine activities. We had both dressed in black clothing and managing to keep our faces hidden, we slipped through the village unseen. He led the way into a shaded dense grove of trees and I felt the first prickling of real fear, until I saw that he had led me to where two magnificent black horses were tethered, hidden from view of the main track. "Where are the others ?" I whispered, my anxiety now suddenly dawning into excitement and I could feel the blood thrumming throughout my body, making me feel more alive than I had in years. "They're already down on the shore waiting for us. There's less likelihood of us being caught, if we spend as much time apart as we can." Within seconds we were astride our mounts and heading towards the open expanse of water. The beast's hooves had been covered in heavy sacking so they made as little noise as possible, but every dull thud made my nerves start to jangle. I had been confident about this, alone in my cottage, but now that it was real, I felt my resolve starting to waiver, I hadn't ridden in years and despite my reservations, I found that I rather enjoyed the opportunity to prove my prowess astride the gentle giant. The breeze over the open fields, was even stronger as we neared the shore. The wind swept straight across from the English Channel from the shores of France and up over the dunes towards us, making my hair fly wildly around my face. Keeping my head low to avoid the buffeting, I gritted my teeth and concentrated on following my guide. Leading me towards a copse we quickly tethered them to the thick trunks until we'd need them later.

Hunched over to avoid any lookouts from noticing us, we ran in the darkness to find the others. The sea bubbled angrily, roaring even louder than the wind. As soon as we gained the top of the dunes, I could see the boat in question bobbing on the waves and a line of men, throwing substantial barrels joined with rope over their shoulders and traipsing back up the beach and to the safety of the empty carts. Watching where I walked and dealing with the unevenness of the sand beneath my feet, I followed my mysterious escort towards where the other men waited. Nearing the gang, I saw several of the men stiffen imperceptibly, whilst three of them abandoned their efforts all together, drawing their revolvers and pointing them firmly in our direction. "Easy Michael, it's me James and the woman I told you of." The men swiftly lowered the weapons, though I still felt several pairs of hostile eyes scrutinising me. "You brought the Bembridge Witch then I see," laughed one of the men, easing the tension at my expense. "All I can see, is a group of men with all the time in the world to stand around and gossip like a group of women." I replied tartly. James coughed sharply, but I noticed a smile stealing across his face, his eyes flashing in surprise and admiration, while my words seemed to galvanise the other men back into action. I hadn't ventured out of my hiding hole, just to be seen simply as a frail woman, so making for the nearest barrel, I helped James to push it uphill. The work was arduous, but fear and pride kept me moving and I knew I would need one of my own remedies to heal the blisters come the morning. Each man worked as hard as the next and soon we had the barrels safely loaded onto three carts, carefully covered in straw, safe from prying eyes and it was time to go our separate ways. I stood back and watched in admiration as James speedily attached the horses to one of the carts, with calm expert hands, before slowly trotting them back towards Howgate Lane. I fought the impulse to force the horses into a gallop, we didn't dare to risk drawing attention to ourselves. "Are you pleased that you came along to see where your ill-gotten gains comes from ?" his tone seemed lighter, as if I'd finally proven myself in his eyes and had been judged useful. "I found it thrilling if I'm completely honest."

"It's not quite so thrilling when the revenue inspectors are after you."

"No" I nodded in sombre agreement, terrified at the mere thought of being chased by the revenue men. "What happens now ? Where does it all go ?" The excitement still coursed through my veins and I wanted to know more.

"The carts go to three different hiding places, yours being

one of them. There's less chance of us losing it all if we split it. We try to get as much as we can, but it never seems to be enough to meet the demand. You're doing a great service to the island by helping us, there will be many merry men who would wish to thank you for your sacrifice." I laughed scornfully at his praise. "No one would drink a drop of that brandy if they knew that I had a hand in it. Everyone despises me at the moment."
"Well you can be assured that I'm not one of them." He replied gruffly. We were fast approaching the village, so we curtailed our conversation, determined to remain unnoticed. For a dangerous smuggler, James was definitely also a gentleman and surprisingly, being with him seemed so natural. We returned the horses, along with the cart back in the amongst the trees and once James was satisfied that they wouldn't be discovered, he escorted me to the back door, before being enveloped by the all-consuming darkness. James had explained to me that most of the brandy was distributed around Bembridge, so none of the villagers investigated too closely when they saw anything suspicious. It was an advantageous arrangement on both sides and one that I desperately hoped he would be proved right on, after all if I was arrested for hiding contraband the frustrated villagers would make sure I was punished, especially if they couldn't officially charge me for witchcraft.

On my own in my little bed in the still darkness of the cottage, my dreams were filled with brandy barrels and dark ships bobbing around in the choppy waters, sailing off into the night for unknown destinations. I wanted to accompany James on his next collection, I felt safe when I was with him and something told me that this time he wouldn't object.

Chapter 14

The soft white snow lay thickly on the ground, covering the whole island in a frozen blanket, muffling all sounds and settling on every tree branch, hedge, roof and fence. For a while, I amused myself by watching the children running around outside, whooping and cheering as though they didn't have a care in the world. The boys throwing snowballs backwards and forwards in delight, whilst the girls concentrated their efforts on building a huge snowman between them, complete with his own snow wife and snow children. Winding my shawl tightly around my face and neck, I ventured out of The Hatch, the sound of my footsteps, thankfully absorbed by the silence of the deep layer of snow. I crept around the side of the cottage and spied the children in the distance on the hills above me, speeding down precariously atop sledges, their cheeks as red as the breast of the robin sitting on my wall, watching me warily. I mourned the fact that I was not a child anymore, I was a grown up now and all alone in the world, with the weight of the world on my slender shoulders and I honestly didn't know if I could bear it. When I was little, I would run around on those same hills with Hannah, having fun until the snow soaked through our clothing and we were forced to return home, where our mothers yelled and threatened us with influenza for being so careless and our hands and feet burned in the heat of the fire. "I've got some scraps for you" I whispered to the pigs, momentarily running back inside to fetch the leftovers from lunch. At the first sign of snowflakes, the pigs had hidden themselves away, the aroma of the chicken I proffered, prompted them to chance the cold and they waddled and grunted towards me enthusiastically. "Morning Harriet" the name of the pig making me laugh as it did every time I used it, handing her the choicest pieces of tender chicken. "There you are lazy" I laughed at the second pig. "You'll have to put some effort into it, if you want an equal share of the food." I watched them snuffling around looking for more scraps and becoming annoyed, when they were unable to find any. Sighing, I turned to go back into the cottage, I could just make out muffled footsteps racing around the corner, towards me. Frantically, I pushed the door open, my panic and instinct for self-preservation taking over as I raced to get safely inside before I was discovered. It was only when I heard a thin reedy voice cry out to me, that I froze. "Molly ? Molly can you help ?" Turning around I saw Albert, the young boy from the mill who'd caught me hiding with William so long ago, that it seemed like another lifetime all together. Albert seemed so thinner and taller than when I'd last set eyes upon him and I noted with concern that his perpetual hacking cough was still all too evident. I just had time to close the door before he almost succeeded in pulling me off my feet. "Stop Albert" I commanded, something in my tone successfully cutting through the panic and he slumped heavily against the cottage wall. "You have to come to the mill. One of the lads is in a bad way." Instinctively stepping away from him, I shook my head regretfully, aghast at what he asked of me. "I can't… I can't face them up at the mill. Everyone hates me. Go and find someone else." I turned away from him, but Albert wasn't about to be ignored. "Not everyone hates you Molly. We need you. You have to come, now!" There were tears in his eyes and I remembered how he had kept mine and William's secret and though I had severe doubts about listening to him, I knew my mother would want me to be strong and help if I could, rather than cowering in my bed. "Wait there" I said, disappearing back

into the cottage to grab my emergency bag. Feeling with
shaking fingers that my shawl was still in place, I followed
Albert at a run, swiftly realising that he was leading me
towards the windmill of all places. When I was little, I had
ran around in the snow for fun, but now that it was an
emergency, I found that it was about as easy as running in
wet sand. The snow sucked at our boots as we went and the
damp chill ascended up through my legs, making my teeth
chatter. "So what happened ?" I panted, trying to remain
calm, in the face of Albert's terror. "It's Matthew. The trap
doors were open because one of the doors needed
repairing, he tripped and went right through both sets. He
fell a long way." Swallowing hard, I tried not to distress
him, more than was necessary and decided against asking
any further questions until I could see for myself what I
was dealing with. "We need to hurry." Gritting my teeth in
preparation, my heart pounding in my chest, I was relieved
to find that we'd finally reached the mill. The sails were
weighted down with a thick covering of snow and the
white patchwork of fields spread out below us sparkled
magically in the sunlight. Holding my bag in a vice like
grip I followed young Albert in through the opened
doorway. Immediately in front of me I was faced with a
cluster of men looking down at the floor. Albert weaved in
between the group and motioned for them to stand back.
Gasping in shock as they parted, I saw the figure of a little
boy sprawled on the floor in front of me. Swallowing my
fear, I crept forward and knelt beside his tiny frame. His
eyes were closed but he writhed from side to side,
whimpering in anguished pain. Tears welled in my eyes,
there had been no point in bringing my bag with me, there
was nothing I could do for the young boy. Stretching out a
hand, I gently smoothed his blonde hair. "Matthew" I
whispered soothingly and his eyelids flickered open at the
sound of his own name. He sought me out and I smiled

weakly, for his sake. "I want my mother" he whispered, "I want to tell her it was an accident and that… I'm sorry." "She'll be here soon," I hoped the good Lord wouldn't punish me for telling him a lie. "She'll not be cross with you. Have no fear." I judged him to be around six years of age and my heart felt broken when I thought of how brave he was being, for one so young. "It hurts" he confided. "I know" I said solemnly, resting my hand on top of his. "Close your eyes and your ma will be here soon." I looked pointedly at Albert and as he rushed off back out of the door, I prayed that he would be able to find Matthew's mum before it was too late. Everything inside the mill was still, the helpless men stood around muttering quietly and I sang quiet songs to the boy, ones that my mother used to sing to me when I was little and I tried not to weep at the sorrow of it all. It seemed like hours had passed since Albert had left, though in reality it had only been minutes and I couldn't stop myself from anxiously checking the door every few seconds. As I feared, his breathing suddenly changed, becoming more laboured and he struggled for each breath. "Hold on Matthew" I pleaded. "She's nearly here. Wait for your ma, she'll get here." His eyes opened once again, fixing on me, though I could see they were beginning to lose focus. "Tell her I love her and I'm sorry" he rasped and then he was gone.   "Nooooooo!!!" A drawn out wail made me jump. Matthew's mother had arrived just in time to witness him lose his fight for life. "Why did you allow that evil witch near my poor boy ?" She screamed hysterically. "What were you thinking ?" I stood waiting for one of the men to defend me, but they merely stood mutely looking at me, while Matthew's mother collapsed with grief. Even talkative Albert stood quietly by and said nothing. Grabbing my bag, I swept from the mill with as much dignity as I could muster. I was shaken to the core. I was

151

supposed to be a healer, but I'd failed to relieve Matthew's suffering, though I'd tried my best to offer him comfort in his time of need. I'd made myself go out during the daylight, facing the villagers and just managed to prove that I'd been right to remain in my home. I stumbled blindly through my tears, my feet disappearing into the deep snow and nearly lost my footing several times, as I rushed down the hill towards the safety of my home. The chill seeped into my bones and in the welcoming glow of my own fire, I wept for the little boy who would never play in the snow again.

Chapter 15

It was once again, one of the dark nights in between moons when James came to knock on the back door of the cottage. He'd agreed to my request to take me with him once more. Deep down I knew I should feel nervous, but I was far too excited to have any misgivings. I'd been alone with only my own company night after night for much too long and I was eager to be out once again with the wind flowing through my hair and without having to feel like an outcast in my own village. Opening the door, I placed my head on top of my head and without a word we disappeared into the darkness of the night, before anyone could notice us. I was a little disappointed to find that we wouldn't be riding a horse each, but instead we would be taking the horse and cart directly to the beach this time. "Where are you from ?" I hadn't wanted to pry, but I couldn't help myself, so I waited patiently through an awkward silence before he answered. "I live in Yaverland, but my family come from Nettlestone." This at least explained why I hadn't seen him around Bembridge. "Have you always been in the… supply business ?" Choosing my words carefully so as not to cause any offence at what he did and I didn't want to give him any further excuses to stop talking, now that he was finally opening up to me. "It's a family business, it's all I've ever known. I wouldn't know how to be a respectable gentleman if I tried" he laughed, scornful at the very thought of conforming. As we travelled, we swapped stories about our different childhoods and I found that I enjoyed talking to another adult, I'd spent far too long with only myself and the spiders for company. The fresh breeze increased as we reached the edge of the dunes once more.

Down below us on the beach, I just managed to make out the men, in a line as before, some rolling the large barrels up from the water's edge and others carrying them to the dunes, just below where we sat with one of the carts. Dismounting, James came around to my side, putting his hands firmly on the sides of my waist, lifting me carefully out of the cart, so that when I finally stood on the ground, we were face to face, close enough to kiss had we wanted to. Overcome with embarrassment and confusion, I turned quickly away and we headed towards the others, coming forward to meet us. Since I'd already met the men on my last trip, combined with the fact that I'd invested a large amount of my own money in their last couple of ventures, they accepted me far more readily than they had before. Hurrying down to help, we soon had all of the barrels loaded safely onto the carts. The wind was strong and I had to resort to holding onto my hat, or risk losing it altogether and I couldn't risk leaving anything incriminating behind. We all quickly parted company and four cart loads all set off in their separate directions, whilst we took the final cart back towards the village. The horses trotted along in the darkness and all was well, until we saw a faint yellow light bobbing along mysteriously, further up ahead. James drew the cart to a stop and with a discreet turn of his head, he checked that the black blankets still covered the barrels in the back. "It could be one of the revenue men" he whispered. "Now's your chance to show why I was right to bring you along." We moved slowly forward towards the light, drawing nearer, I made out the flame flickering in the lantern. It appeared that James was right and we were indeed, about to be stopped by one of the dreaded revenue men. "Halt" shouted the man, stepping out directly in front of us, brandishing his lantern aloft. "What's your business out here so late ?" I was relieved that I didn't recognise him, which in turn meant that he wouldn't recognise me

either. I had no wish to be interrogated by someone who was prejudiced against the local witch. "We were just out for a ride" I leapt in, before James could answer, putting my hand on his leg in a subtle but intimate gesture, hoping that this would prove we were a couple. The man spotted the movement, but his eyes wandered towards the back of the cart. I felt James' muscles bunching beneath his shirt in temper, and prayed that he wouldn't be querulous. If we insulted this man or aroused his suspicions, we'd be uncovered. "My mother doesn't like my new beau I'm afraid, so we have to wait until she's asleep before we can be together." I smiled as sincerely as I could muster, though I found it hard to breathe. The man seemed to relax and I thought I'd finally started to win him around. "Henry here, is just waiting for my father to come back from working in Newport, before he asks him for my hand in marriage." Putting my hand across James' shoulders, I pulled his face towards mine, kissing him passionately. His lips were soft and warm and I'd only intended the kiss to be a quick show of affection for the revenue man's benefit, but James responded in kind and we were soon lost in the moment. It was only when the man coughed, that we remembered where we were and quickly broke apart. "I'll let you two be alone, be careful how you go. There're rogues that travel these roads at night time you know." The man waved us indulgently on and we both tried to look suitably worried at the prospect of running into any ruffians, holding our breath until we were safely out of sight of the kindly yet gullible, revenue man. "You were amazing!" James laughed, shaking his head in wonder. "You definitely proved your worth tonight Mol." I grinned smugly, but my hands had begun to shake slightly, as the shock took over. "I'm glad you think so."
"If not for you, he would've checked the back. You were very convincing." He looked at me questioningly out of the

corner of his eye. "So were you." I shot back tartly, giggling at our daring, in the face of such danger. James stopped the cart at the side of the cottage, safely out of view of the neighbouring cottages and we rolled the barrels quietly into their hiding place, trying not to disturb the pigs. "Would you like to come in for a nip of brandy ? It's getting colder by the minute out here ?" Without waiting for an answer, I led the way into the cottage, relieved that James followed, taking his ease in a seat in front of the blazing fire. I felt a rare frisson of excitement as I regarded him, in my tiny room. He seemed so at ease and I'd never witnessed a man, stretching his long legs out in front of the hearth before. The Hatch had been full of too many women and few men I'd dared to hope that James might just be the man to change it. I marvelled at how familiar we'd become with one another, since our first meeting, when he'd rudely forced his way into my home and I hadn't even been able to see his face. My hands fumbled and I filled his cup with more brandy than I'd originally intended. "So you decide to seduce me in the cart and now you're trying to get me drunk, was this your wicked plan all along ?" I jumped, as I realised he was standing directly behind me. "Your drink sir" handing him the brandy, I shot him an innocent smile. "Will you join me ?" Tossing back the drink in one go, I felt the fire making its way down through my body, warming me from the inside. I hadn't realised before how grey his eyes were and his close proximity, made my insides melt with a pure longing I'd never experienced before. When William had propositioned me so long ago, I'd rejected him because of my morals, but now I knew what happened to women who resisted and I was determined not to lose James to another woman, though for all I knew, he could already have a wife waiting at home in Yaverland for him. After so many years of living in fear, I was exhausted with trying to do the right thing and thinking of others, it was high time I thought of my own needs for once. Throwing caution to the wind, I took James by the hand, leading him back to the chair, motioning for him to sit in front of the hearth once more. He raised an eyebrow at me in quizzical amusement, running a hand through his short sandy hair, but he complied with my orders all the same and seated himself, with the empty brandy cup still in his hands. Standing in front of him, I carefully unbuttoned my blouse, starting at the neck and slowly working all the way down, until I could shrug myself out of the garment before throwing it on the floor at my feet. Next, I freed myself from the thick folds of my voluminous skirt and stood before him, in nothing but my tightly laced corset. Without a word, James slowly stood, he didn't take his stormy eyes off mine for a second, while he reached behind me untying my stays, letting it fall on top of the pile of clothes I'd already discarded. Shuddering in delight, as his gaze took in my naked body from top to bottom, I revelled in the frank approval reflected in his eyes. As he kissed me, we collapsed onto the floor in front of the roaring flames and I shivered as his lips moved lower onto my neck and we made love by the flickering flames of several candles and the roaring fire. Only when our desires had been well and truly sated we moved to my bedroom, where we began the process all over again. The following morning, as the bright morning sun shone through the windows, I lay in James' arms, content but a little sore, I'd expected as much and already had a jar of ointment on hand to lessen the irritation, once James had left. I'd heard many stories from girls I knew, about their first time and I'd been fully prepared for it to be an awkward and uncomfortable experience, which I'd heard got better and more enjoyable with practice, but my first time had been pleasurable and satisfying and if it was going to become even better when repeated, then I wanted

157

to do it a lot more. Moving my head slightly I grimaced as the motion disturbed him and his eyes flew open, searching for me. "Sorry" I whispered, kissing him on his forehead and we lay in silence, simply looking at one another. I'd once allowed myself to believe that I'd been in love with William Gould, but now I knew it had been nothing more than an infatuation borne out of a young girl's fantasy. The easy companionship, I felt with James was something I'd never experienced with a man before and he was definitely not an adolescent boy. William had been just eighteen when I'd first fallen for him, I judged James to be around thirty and the difference between them was striking. Whilst William was full of his own self-importance and eager to prove himself to everyone, James had a quiet aura of command and capability about him, which I found alluring, making me feel safe in a way that even my father had never managed to do. "I want to invest more money on the next run." I suddenly blurted out, wanting to be more involved with him on every level possible. "Straight down to business I see." He murmured, with his habitual lazy smile that I now found endearing. I blushed slightly, "sorry, would you like something to eat ?"

"Not yet" he grinned slyly, "I need to build up an appetite first." After several more tumbles in my bed, I eventually managed to extricate myself from his arms and staggered downstairs. My hair was awry and my lips were puffed and sore from James' insistent kisses, but I no longer cared. By the time James came down to join me, there were eggs cooked to perfection, fluffy bread slathered in thick golden butter and cups of strong tea, laid out on the table waiting for him. Looking around the room in frustration, I decided that I'd have to do something about cleaning the place up. "My my, this is a feast, I should enjoy waking up to this every morning." At his words, I choked on the tea I'd been trying to daintily sip, whilst he sat with an amused look on his face, watching me in return. "I hope that wasn't on my account" he laughed, slipping a runny yolk on a hunk of buttered bread and devouring it whole. "Do you not have someone waiting for your return ?" I asked uncertainly, terrified of hearing the answer. Shaking his head, he drank his hot tea. "I've never felt the need to get myself involved with a woman… before." Smiling happily, I curbed the instinct to grab him and refuse to ever let him leave The Hatch. "I do need to go and check and visit some patrons, but I could come back later if you wanted me to ?" Nodding mutely, unable to believe my luck at the handsome man that God had provided for me. I was determined not to get carried away with romantic notions like I had before, but I couldn't deny that I had a good feeling about myself and James. There was only one regret that I had and it was that I'd waited so many years before experiencing the pleasure of love making. "The next time there's a run to France, I want to invest more money." The events of last night had filled me with confidence about our venture and I wanted to prove to him, that I believed in his ability to make us money. "I'm looking for more backers for the next trip. It's our most ambitious yet, we could make more money than all the rest of the ventures so far this year."

"When will it happen ?" I asked, drawing my knees up to my chest and wrapping my arms tightly around my legs, while luxuriating in the deliciousness of having a companion to discuss things with, across the table in the morning. "Are you sure you want to do this ?" I'd never been more certain about anything in my whole life. I knew my father wouldn't have approved and that only seemed to spur me on. I was taking control of my own life, for once and it felt good. I stood and retrieved a purse, deliberately showing him the place where I kept all my wealth. "Here" I said, throwing the heavy purse containing all of my savings, except for a few shillings I always kept beneath my bed for emergencies. Letting out a low whistle, James weighed the amount in his hand. "I promise you a good return on this. You'll want for nothing after this." He assured me, leaning forward and kissing me gently on the tip of my nose. "I have to go. I'll be back at nightfall." I saw him to the door and found to my surprise that I missed him, the minute he'd left the cottage. This was the relationship I'd been waiting for all my life and it was difficult to accept that I might have the chance of a happy ending after all. "Harriet's welcome to that young boy, William Gould" I shouted at the top of my voice, dancing happily around the cottage.

Chapter 16

The weather outside was particularly inclement, especially
for my beloved island, which usually had more than its fair
share of sunshine and as a consequence, us villagers tried
not to venture outside if we could help it on such days.
Without being able to tend my vegetable and herb patch, I
was kept busy inside the cottage for several days making
up remedies and tinctures to relieve the Bembridge
inhabitants of their coughing and shivering symptoms. My
supplies were still being anonymously purchased on my
behalf, so I passed the time, working happily in the still
room. My wealth had grown into a considerable sum and
before I'd passed it over to James, I would sit and count it
all, every evening with an almost obsessive preoccupation.
Having money, meant that I wouldn't have to feel scared
any more, it was protection, surety that I would never have
to go begging from neighbours who were suspicious and
scared of me, or ending up in the Newport workhouse,
which was always in the back of every person's mind. It
was a symbol of my faith in him that I'd entrusted
everything to him and he assured me that the next run
would be their largest haul, I would be a rich woman and
all I had to do was wait for two weeks. I fancied that we
might even move to Sandown, where no one knew us and
we could start afresh, my dreams of our future kept me
entertained as I worked, making it difficult to concentrate.

One night, there was a soft knocking at the back door and
although he'd told me he was visiting various inns on
business and wouldn't see me until late, my first thought
was that it would be James. He'd spent every night with me
since we'd first made love and we'd found an easy

companionship and deep love for one another. I hoped that he'd finished his meetings early and had rushed home to me. Flying down the stairs and snatching open the door expectantly, it took me several minutes to gain my composure, when I found a complete stranger at the door instead. At first I suspected it might be one of the customs officers, but I realised that if that were the case, he would have knocked on the front door and not at the back. Thrown, I resisted the strong impulse to slam the door in his face and decided to stand and take the measure of him instead. The man was only slightly taller than I was, with sandy coloured hair and a thin moustache. His deep brown eyes were kindly and creased from habitual laughter and he seemed harmless. "My apologies for disturbing you Miss Downer. I'm the Reverend Henry Thompson and I've been meaning to call on you for some time, but I've found myself rather busy of late, I do hope you'll forgive me." I gasped, feeling like I'd been punched violently in the stomach, as I recognised the man who'd inadvertently told me about my father's death, without realising who I was. But now I was face to face with my father's replacement and he knew me for my father's daughter. This invader was a traitor, a usurper to my father's recently vacated throne, yet something about him made my hand freeze on the door, I found myself liking him despite my better judgement. Sensing that I was at least willing to hear him out, Henry continued, "I know that you don't like to answer your front door any longer and I'm also aware that you don't like to be outside during the day. I don't normally call at a lady's home so late at night, especially calling at the back door, so I hope you'll excuse me." Too embarrassed to invite him into my home, I grabbed a shawl "shall we take the evening air ?" Walking slowly through the village made me nervous at first but the men passing us by on their way back from the inn, were too deep in their cups to pay any attention to two figures, slipping slowly through the evening darkness. The weather had turned mild and I found it quite pleasing to be out at night with the light breeze cooling the heavy hair fastened into a bun at my neck. Bats swooped overhead and cats ran across our path chasing unseen enemies as we walked and began to get to know each other. His actual title was the Reverend Sir Henry Thompson, 3rd Baronet of Virkees. Despite his aristocratic background, I was surprised to find that he was very down to earth and I was sure that my father would approve of him as his replacement. Entering the empty churchyard I followed him to the chapel door and reluctantly accepted his invitation to step inside. Candles burned brightly on the altar and breathing in deeply, I tried to suppress my conflicting emotions as they threatened to engulf me. The last time I'd stood in the nave of the chapel, my father had been alive and now I didn't even have a grave to visit to pay my respects or talk to him when I needed advice. Anger briefly fought with sorrow, but eventually I managed to set my features into a placid mask and turned to smile at Henry. He motioned for me to sit and waited silently whilst I settled myself one a pew, normally reserved for the likes of the Dennetts. "How are you Molly ?" His words took me back a little, no one had asked me that question for as long as I could remember. My mouth began to form a meaningless platitude, but despite myself and for a reason that I couldn't quite fathom, I found myself being honest with this strange man, resembling my father so strongly in his caring manner. "I don't know, to be perfectly honest. I've felt very angry both at God and the world and I feel that the best way to deal with those feelings, is to remain safely inside my home and not see anyone. Though now it's got to the point where it's not just my feelings that count, now I'm in hiding from the villagers who believe I'm a witch." He considered my words for a while, without making any snap judgements and that raised him even higher in my estimation than he'd been before. Candlelight both illuminated and produced shadows resembling little demons, dancing on the high vaulted ceiling. I pulled my shawl tighter to her body, shuddering at the images. "Are you happy with the way things are ?" Biting my lip, I considered the question. "I wasn't for such a long time, but I truly feel that I'm healed now."

"If you didn't want to visit me here during the daytime, you could always meet me here in the evening, after everyone else has left and we could pray together or read from the bible if you would find that comforting." I smiled, relieved to be accepted by this new incomer to the village, when everyone else had turned against me. "You know" I said with a deep heartfelt appreciation. "I might just take you up on that offer."

"What was your father like ?" He asked suddenly. "I know he was well regarded here, but what was the man himself like ?" Smiling in spite of the pain, as my father's face swam into view, I tried to explain to a stranger, how much my pa had meant to me. "It's hard for me to be objective, because I loved him so very much." I stared at the candles orange and yellow flame as it danced in front of my eyes. "He was just so very kind. He always had time for anyone who had need of him, even though he had many responsibilities in other areas. He made you feel as if you were the most important person in the whole world." My head dropped and I stared at my shaking hands. If I'd been one of the other village ladies, I might have worn gloves, but I eschewed most of society's conventions and my fine white hands, glistened like ivory in the light of the dimly lit church. "Thank you" was all Henry said abruptly standing, pulling me out of my nostalgic reverie. "Let me escort you home, it's late for a young woman to be out of her home."

Walking back towards the cottage there were far fewer people around and I could hear the sea, lashing itself angrily against the shoreline out of sight. Shuddering, I imagined the fear of being onboard a tiny boat sailing from France, doing their best to try and dodge the revenue cutters sailing mercilessly up and down the stretch of water. Finally, we reached my door and Henry stopped, bestowing a dazzling smile on me. "Thank you for your company, if you don't seek me out, then I promise that I shall come and seek you out, for you cannot shut yourself away from the whole of the world." As he made to leave, he turned and lowered his voice whispering, "take care Molly Downer, it was lovely to meet you. I do hope to see you again soon." His voice was full held a note of genuine concern, but I didn't reply, I merely closed the door gently. I honestly didn't know if I would take Henry up on his offer to talk, but as I settled in front of the fire to wait for James, my tread felt lighter for the first time in months, it was good to know that someone else in the village was on my side after all.

Chapter 17

Abraham Boyes stepped forward and raised his arm, waiting for the crowd to quieten down. Tensions were beginning to fray and someone needed to take charge of those who had assembled in the Olde Village Inne. It was such an important gathering that even women had been permitted to enter. "We all know that something has to be done about Molly Downer. We've to decide how we wish to proceed." His words were like a revolver being fired and the crowd exploded in anger. "She is a witch and we need to drive her out of the village as soon as possible." Shouted one voice, at the very back of the room, followed by a loud noise of agreement. "We will have to provide proof if we want something done about her." Abraham said warningly. "We have to tread carefully since they made trials of witches illegal."

"But we've just suffered several years of drought and that's had a terrible effect on our crops. Surely that's proof that we have a witch in the village. They have to listen to us if we have proof don't they ?" The crowd erupted in agreement once more and Abraham, the much respected baker found it hard to disagree with them. He'd seen at first hand the terrible harvests over the past few years, it was no wonder that the villagers were angry and afraid. "Is there anything else we can use ?" He asked, trying to regain order once more whilst making sure that his wife was managing to write down the charges being made against Molly Downer. "She's used sorcery to seduce our new reverend, so she can use the chapel for her own private communication with the devil," voiced one reedy voice at the front, full of passion if not volume and several of the women nodded their heads in agreement. "I'm not sure what she does in that chapel" Mrs Tyrell piped up, "but I'm very uncomfortable with the relationship she's struck up with Henry Thompson, even though none of us have set eyes on her in years." Abraham smiled in encouragement at the indignant Mrs Tyrell, nodding at his wife to include her objection in her notes. "I seen her dancing around her vegetable patch, naked as the day she was born, beneath the full moon" shouted one man, as another male voice shouted in response, "lucky you, I know where I'll be on the next full moon then" and most of the men collapsed into laughter, clapping the speaker on his shoulder good naturedly, whilst the women scowled disapprovingly. "All right, all right that is enough please gentlemen. We do have ladies present" commanded Abraham Boyes, trying to keep order. "We've had nought but sour milk for nigh on three weeks" complained one voice, "my cake refused to rise" said another.

"My husband caught sight of her and was struck down with the pox two weeks later" yelled another. Mrs Boyes kept her head bent as she struggled to keep up with the various testimonies. "Very well" said Abraham, satisfied with the evidence they'd gathered. "I shall take these notes to the Brading Mayor and see what he has to say, hopefully he'll take the matter further and rid us of this malign influence in our otherwise happy village. Ladies I thank you for your time, you may return to your homes and your children now."

Chapter 18

Each day, the weather appeared to be warmer and the nights lighter for a little longer each evening. When my father died, I'd never thought I would set foot in the chapel ever again, but Reverend Thompson had changed my thinking and now I could even see that there might be a time when I might visit the chapel once more in daylight. I had been secretly harbouring a dream of James proposing for some months and now it might even be possible for us to be married in our own chapel and I thought of how proud my mother and father would have been and how painful it would be, to marry without them beside me. I'd been to visit Henry several times a week recently and not always so late in the evening. He'd given me the confidence to step out at twilight and every now and again I would feel mischievous so I'd leave the cottage a little earlier, another reason for my earlier visits was my eagerness to get back home and wait for James to return. On the whole, if I saw anyone from the village, most people simply made the sign of protection against the evil eye, but so far, no one had jeered at me or thrown anything in my direction, I was relieved and a little encouraged. 'Surely a good Christian community can find it in them to show some forgiveness' I thought to myself on more than one occasion. Once, on my way home I saw Hannah and she definitely seemed thicker around the middle and I couldn't prevent the corners of my mouth twitch knowingly. I'd even halfheartedly swept the besom across the floor for the first time in many months, James had all but moved in with me, yet I'd still allowed cobwebs to hang from the beams and thick dust lining every surface.

So far, I'd managed to prevent the good reverend from stepping inside my home, I didn't want the only village person who accepted me, to be horrified at my living arrangements, but my pride wasn't enough to motivate me into thoroughly cleaning the cottage. I also wanted to prevent him from finding out that I was living in sin with a man who made his money from brandy smuggling. I'd lived in this way for so long, that it was difficult to remember a time when my home had ever been clean. The only pangs of guilt that I ever felt, were when I thought of my mother and what she would make of her lovely pristine home, looking more like a hovel, but once again it failed to provide sufficient inducement for me to change matters and until James declared that he was unhappy with the accommodation I doubted that much would alter my mind on the subject. My temper had mellowed with the help of the new reverend and his willingness to listen to anything that I wished to confide in him, he was the next best thing to having my father with me. I was so moved by the generosity of his spirit, that without him knowing, I wrote a will, leaving my house and any monies to Henry, to help the church and the poor of the parish, once I'd passed on. I no longer visited the windmill at night, but spent my time happily with James at home instead.

One morning, I decided that it was high time for me to take the poppets out of the chimney breast. Although they didn't bother me on a daily basis, I still thought of them now and again and whenever I did I was filled with shame of what James or Reverend Henry Thompson would make of them if they knew. Fumbling in the chimney breast, I pulled out the soot covered figures, which I'd placed there so long ago. Looking at them, I remembered the anger, but with a sense of detachment. Tracing their minute features with my thumb, I was so absorbed in them that when I heard the stew bubbling over, I absent mindedly threw the figures into the window, near where I sat. Hurrying over to deal with the catastrophe, I left the poppets in the window to be dealt with later. As the sun began to set over the island I finished my second bowl of warming stew, left some for James' supper and went to retrieve the figures. I planned to carefully take them apart, by unwrapping them and undoing the curses, before burying them safely underneath a waning moon, ensuring that no one would ever know they had even existed. Sadly, I regarded them and thought about the path my life might have taken, had not circumstances intervened. Henry had told me that Harriet still had no ability to walk or talk and I wondered whether he blamed me like everyone else did and resolved to talk to him about it, later in the evening. I even thought that I might tell him about the poppets and hoped that he would be proud of me, for disposing of them, it was a clear sign of how far I'd come. It was a warm night so I'd left the door slightly ajar for James to lock on his return, but as I held the poppets, the back door suddenly flew open and Hannah strode forcefully into the cottage, filling the small room with her presence. It was the first time we'd faced one another in many years and the cottage crackled with the tension. Cursing myself for feeling secure enough to leave myself vulnerable to visitors, I tried in vain to conceal the little figures, but it was too late.

I watched Hannah's face draining of all its colour, instantly nervous that she might faint onto the floor in front of me. "I cannot believe my own eyes. Even though the whole village said that it was true, I told them all that they were wrong. I said that you would not be so evil and yet here you are as bold as brass." The green of her bonnet, gave her a strange tint which served to make her seem even more queasy and I motioned for her to sit down. "What do you mean the whole village ? What are they asking ?" I demanded in panic, as Hannah unsteadily seated herself in front of the fire, placing her head in her hands. "Joe noticed those wicked little creatures first, though heaven knows how he managed it, through the grime of your windows. People have been walking past all afternoon trying to find out if it's true. They were sorely afraid of you before, but now the villagers are scared and angry and they're demanding to have you charged as a witch. Every time there's a drought, or a cake fails to rise or even when the milk curdles you get the blame, but this... what you've done is beyond all of that."

"I had no idea" I whispered aghast. "I was disposing of these stupid poppets for once and for all. I'm not angry at everyone any longer. I've had enough of feeling so filled with this hate. Henry Thompson has been helping me. I even have a new beau, I no longer feel anything for William Gould, I've just been trying to live quietly here in my own home." My voice took on a pleading tone, as I realised the predicament I found myself in. If they did manage to get the law against witchcraft implemented once more, they could ask the authorities to charge me as a witch, I could be set alight, hung, drowned or even die slowly in a jail somewhere on the mainland and the thought terrified me to my very core, my mother and I had spent all our lives trying to protect ourselves from such horrors. "Let me see those... those evil things." Hannah commanded, her brown eyes flashing in warning, lest I dared to disobey. Handing them over I avoided my old friend's eyes, I couldn't bear to see the hatred in them where once had been such friendship and understanding, there was only betrayal and pain. Hannah looked at the figures in distaste, but when she saw the one that resembled her, she gasped in shock. "This one is... it is me is it not ?" Miserably, I nodded. "This version of me, has a swollen stomach, but how could you know about that ?" When I didn't answer, Hannah leapt forward, grabbing me hard around the wrists,

171

her voice rising in anger. "Answer me. How could you know ?" My voice sounded strangled as I heard myself confessing something I'd previously been too ashamed or angry to admit, to myself let alone anyone else. "I wished for it." Hannah snorted in derision, maintaining her firm hold on my wrists. Keeping her voice low and level while confusion flickered in her eyes, I could tell Hannah was struggling with the dark secrets she had unwittingly uncovered. "Why would you wish for me to be pregnant ? Why ?" Pulling myself free, I massaged my sore red wrists and realised my sorrow had reached a new low. I knew that there was no longer any use in hiding anything and no point in being defensive, thanks to Henry Thompson and the happiness that James gave me, meant that all my fight had left me and there was only room for apologies and remorse. "I was so distraught and angry at the course you'd decided upon with that married man, that I wished that you would become pregnant, so that you would be alone and shamed in front of the whole village. I'm sorry Hannah, truly I am, but I was so angry at the sin you were committing, you and that despicable married man of yours." With the speed of a cat, attacking its prey, Hannah leapt forward, slapping me soundly across the face, making my head snap back painfully. "What would a benevolent and loving God, a God who punishes a woman for merely being in love with a man, a man trapped in an unhappy marriage, make of a witch, who makes dolls of people and curses them ? Do you really not think that your own sin is even worse than my own ?" She spat.

In all of my actions, I'd always told myself that God fully approved of my deeds, but when Hannah laid everything out before me, try as I might, I couldn't remember my reasoning and started to quake at the enormity of what I'd done. "Malcom's died Molly" Hannah whispered, as I slumped down ungainly into the chair opposite her. I wanted to say how sorry I was, that I would take it back if I could, but I couldn't find the words and I merely sat, dissolving into gulping sobs instead. "I may have lost him, but I'm carrying his child and I am shamed. I'm leaving the village before anyone else finds out. If the others do come after you, that's your own affair. You've brought this evil upon yourself, whatever happens now, it is all your own fault. I'm not the only one who is shamed in front of the whole of Bembridge, but mark my words, you'll be the only one who is shamed and alone, for I will at least have my child to love me." Rising, Hannah swept imperiously from the cottage, with her burgeoning stomach visible from beneath her dress. I wanted to shout after her, that I wouldn't be alone, that I had James, but I doubted she would believe me and if Hannah was going to leave the village it wouldn't matter anyway. 'Let her have the last word' I thought to myself, trying to be more charitable after all the terrible things I'd done. I had much greater things to worry about now. I needed to know how serious the threat from the villagers was. James and I may have to move to Sandown quicker than I'd planned, to escape the hostile villagers and their charges of witchcraft. I wanted to know where Hannah would go, now that she would be forced to bring a child up all alone. She didn't come from a wealthy family who could give her money or a home to start her new life and she didn't have a skill like my mother had, to keep them from the workhouse, but I knew that I was the last person she'd confide in, so without another word, I let her sweep out of my home for the last time.

Throwing another log on the fire, I shuddered as I imagined gentle, kind Hannah in Newport's poorhouse. I resolved to speak to Henry, to intervene on my behalf and speak to the villagers about dropping their campaign to have me tried as a witch. Pouring a large measure of brandy to settle my nerves, I sat waiting in front of the fire for James' return. When my hands had regained their usually steadiness, I pulled some sewing out and began to work on one of his shirts that needed repairing after he ripped a hole in it, trying to evade one of the revenue men. He'd left earlier to collect the brandy, it was the biggest ever haul and once it had all been sold, we would be rich at last, more money than we'd ever dreamed of and we'd finally be able to move home, before the villagers came for me. My head had just started to nod, when there came a heavy pounding on the back door. I told myself that it was probably just a neighbour desperately needing my help, that they'd taken it upon themselves to speak to me directly, whilst another voice told me that perhaps it might be an angry mob, come to burn me for witchcraft. So many thoughts passed through my mind in the few steps it took me to reach the door.

Outside, I saw the grey face flickering in the light from the lantern hung on my wall, of a man I recognised, but couldn't quite place. "I had to see you. James made me come." As if hit by a thunderbolt, I realised that the man was familiar, because I'd seen him on the beach when I'd gone to collect the brandy barrels with James the night we'd first kissed and lain together. My knees buckled, as I realised that if he were not able to come to me himself, there was something drastically wrong. "Where is he ? Where's James ?" The man clutched his side, holding onto the wall in support, his breath came in short ragged bursts. "He was shot. They were waiting for us on the beach. Once we saw them it was too late. James and I tried to run away, but he was shot in the back. He told me to get away and find you, just before he died."

"No!" a wild keening sound burst from my mouth and I wanted to scratch his mouth out for telling such wicked lies, it couldn't be true, it couldn't, we had our whole future before us. "I need to see him." Wiping my eyes, I

174

rose to my feet, ready to run to wherever James was. "You can't" he gasped. "They've taken the bodies, along with the brandy. Everything's gone. I need to get back to my wife." Under any other circumstances I would have offered to help him, after all, James' friend was clearly badly injured himself, but nothing mattered any longer. I'd lost the man I truly loved, I'd lost my future, my chance to have children, to be happy and less importantly I'd also lost every penny I had, apart from the handful of shillings under my bed. Everything my mother and I had worked for, for years, all the money that my father had seen fit to leave me, it was all gone, but the only thing I truly mourned for, was my James. Apart from the money, the other perk of being in business with smugglers, happened to be the free bottles of brandy and I tried to fill the void of my loss and the unremitting pain by drowning my sorrows. As soon as one bottle had been emptied, I merely reached for another. I hadn't eaten since yesterday and didn't feel even slightly hungry. The pain in my stomach that had started as a small discomfort, was now a raging white hot pain and I had no remedy or inclination to relieve my own symptoms. Through the haze, I spotted the poppets which I'd left on the seat following my confrontation with Hannah and wept afresh for all I'd lost. I lay on the floor, reluctant to move, reluctant to live. I'd lost everyone that had ever meant anything to me and no longer had the will left to carry on. I didn't want to live in a world without James.

Chapter 19

Lucy Conway went to the stool in Molly's back garden as she usually did, but for the first time she found only rotting vegetables and the religious texts that she had left the week before were not waiting for her, as they usually were. She banged on the door, which she had never dared to do before, but no answer came. This was not totally a cause for her concern given that Molly had become a hermit, but nevertheless, she could feel her anxiety rising by degrees, something was wrong. Rushing around to the front of the house, she peered in through the black dirty windows which were thick with grime and could just make out two legs, lying on the floor. Lucy ran shrieking through the street, drawing neighbouring women and children to their doors, to see what was happening. Their cottages were all topped with a thick thatch and when someone made such a racket, it was normally to warn that there was a fire and so everyone was instantly alert. "Molly Downer's cottage, come quick" she yelled and word spread throughout the village quicker than a fire through dried grass. Joseph came at a run and two of his apprentices were summarily dispatched to find Henry Thompson. Being the village blacksmith, Joe possessed an impressive strength and he managed to break Molly's front door as easily as snapping a twig in two, consequently making him the first person to have stepped through it in years. Most of the village piled in behind him and each of them stopped as they saw Molly's body on the floor. Her clothing was untouched and she looked as though she were asleep. Joe crept forward, calling her name over and over, but as he touched her hand he could feel her unnatural coldness, her limbs had stiffened in death. "Check her for the witch's mark" came the voice of Abraham Boyes and there were strong mutters of agreement amongst the assembled throng. Most were as superstitious as Abraham and two of the village men stole forward and began stripping Molly's body of its clothes. Had it been any other female body, there would have been outcries of disgust, especially amongst the women, but they were each of them convinced that this was no ordinary woman, this was a witch and on her they would find the devil's mark, the undisputable proof of their accusations. At first, the disrobing was gentle, but it soon became a frenzied attack as their search finally proved fruitless. "Look for her money" shouted Harriet Morey's mother "and give it to my poor daughter for being so afflicted by the witch's curse for all these years." Once again there was agreement from the mob, that grew larger by the minute and they spread out, filling the whole of the cottage, searching every nook and cobwebbed cranny, but once again, they were left disappointed. Lucy Conway who had always believed in Molly and had been the one to find her body, was also the one who found Molly's will in the stillroom and she slipped it quickly into her pocket, so she could pass it to the reverend when he appeared. She had the feeling that with the mood inside the cottage was about to ignite and if they discovered it, the will would be ripped into a hundred pieces. Fortunately, Henry Thompson himself soon appeared. He'd been inside the chapel rather than out visiting parishioners and Joe's lads had easily tracked him down. He was used to delivering sermons and he used the same commanding voice in the tiny room. "What in God's name do you think you're all doing ?" His tone and his authority as a holy man, seemed to break the powerful spell that had bound the crowd in a fever of shared lunacy. "You" he shouted, pointing at one of the village women, "and you" looking at another "clothe this good woman in the way that you found her." Ignoring their scared expressions, he turned on the men "what is the meaning of this ?" Abraham Boyes stepped forward, still the leader, but more pious than he had been previously. "We were looking for the devil's mark upon her that is all reverend, I can assure you."

"and...?" asked Henry with undisguised disgust, tapping his foot with impatience. Hanging his head, Abraham admitted "we found none father." Henry nodded, as if this were an obvious answer. "What were you all doing, wandering around her house ? What else were you looking to find ?"

"We were searching for her money, so we could give it to my Harriet," piped up the recalcitrant Mrs Morey, her grey curls sticking out from under her cap, her chin jutted out in defiance and her ruddy face a mask of indignation.

"And...?" he asked again,

"and we found nothing, nothing at all for my poor girl. We've had to feed her and care for her for all these years all because of that witch." Winding herself into a fury, Mrs Morey spat on the floor in disgust, only narrowly avoiding Molly's body, which was now fully clothed once more. "Out NOW. All of you." He yelled at them, glaring at them as they left one by one.

The last to leave was Lucy Conway, she had been circling near the door, trying not to arouse suspicion in the others. "I found this" she said and passed him the will. Lucy caught hold of his arm, forcing him to look at her, "she was a good woman reverend... really she was" taking one final look at Molly's body still lying on the floor, she heard him whisper "I know," as she walked out of the cottage, unable to see through her tears.

Chapter 20

There was no moon and the dense cover of cloud obscured the stars, making the night a deep black. It was the very dead of night and the villagers, their pets and their livestock were all sleeping soundly. The inn had long since closed and in a few hours the sun would rise over the island, heralding a new day, the village was usually deserted at this time of night, but if anyone had looked out of their windows, they wouldn't have made out the three men stood outside The Hatch. Someone had already daubed the words 'Witches Hatch' across the door, making one of the men chuckle. "Looks like we're not the only ones that were glad to see the death of the witch" he whispered in satisfaction. "She's been dead a week now, it's time to rid Bembridge of any reminders of the scourge she brought on our community." The other two nodded. "Ready ?" Once again, they nodded in agreement, but they froze in unison, as a large owl flew out of the trees to their right, making straight for them. "Do it now" one of the men ordered, struggling to keep his voice calm. "Before she sends more of her familiars to stop us." All three held their torches aloft, so that the flames reached the lower parts of the thatched roof and within seconds the fire had caught. Yellow and orange flames tore through the dry thatch with ease and plumes of black smoke filled the air. "We need to go before anyone sees us." Turning to run, one stopped in panic, staring at the furnace, "we should warn the others, just in case" He whispered urgently. "Not unless we want to get caught, come on, we've got to get home, before anyone sees us." Just as quickly as they had appeared, the men were enveloped by the darkness of the night, unseen. By the time the villagers were stirring, the trails of smoke were still escaping from the cottage. There was nothing left to save, the fire had done its work. There had been little wind and fortunately it had not travelled to any nearby properties and for that they were all thankful. "Who do you think did it ?" Lucy Conway asked, turning to Henry Thompson, as they stood next to the duck pond surveying the scar that had once been a beautiful home. "I'm not sure we will ever find that out, I think we should just focus on the future now. Hopefully we can rebuild the cottage and it will be perfect once more." Lucy smiled at his words, though she was still shocked at the savage attack in their sleepy little village. "I truly hope so" she whispered.

Chapter 21

The Reverend Sir Henry Thompson and Lucy Conway were the only people to witness Molly being interred in her final resting place. She had once confided in Henry that she longed to be buried in St Mary's Church at Brading, near to her mother and away from the Bembridge villagers who had shunned her. When she'd told him of her wish, he had put it to the back of his mind, not expecting to have to arrange her burial, so soon after and had made sure her wishes were honoured. She'd explained that it was the first church that she had ever worshipped in and it had been a place that she'd always loved and felt at home in. She'd also added ruefully, with a smile. "At least I might be granted eternal rest there, I doubt I would have any peace if I were left in Bembridge." The memory of her words, filled him with remorse for a life and a friend lost far too early. He knew that the villagers had disapproved when they'd found out that he had been paying visits to The Hatch and that he had encouraged Molly to privately worship in the chapel at night. They didn't think it seemly that she should be allowed in a holy place and though he had argued that God loved all his children equally and they had no proof for their accusations, he had still been unable to convert anyone to see things his way. Henry had paid out of his own money for a small piece of stone to mark the grave, in the north side of the picturesque little churchyard. It was nothing grand, but he was adamant that she could not be buried in a nameless grave as though she were a no one, as though she had never existed. As he watched her coffin disappear into the ground, Lucy Conway grasped his hand, weeping into her handkerchief, "farewell my little Molly" she sobbed and turned to leave the churchyard. "Good night Bembridge Witch," he smiled "may God bless you."

Epilogue

Mrs Morey came into the cottage and sighed, as she looked at her son. "Any change ?" She asked, as she always did and though it was more out of habit, rather than hope, she felt that not to ask would signal that she'd given up on her daughter making a recovery and she wasn't willing to do that, ever.

Molly Downer had been dead for three years and her house had been burnt to the ground shortly after. The cottage had been rebuilt and now the newly named Myrtle Cottage stood on the site, just behind the little duck pond with a fresh coat of paint gleaming in the sun. A man who owned his own oyster fishing business, had bought Myrtle Cottage for himself, his wife and his three children and they had absorbed themselves into the village well. They'd donated generously to the chapel and employed a handful of men and boys to work for them, for which the Bembridge inhabitants were grateful. If anyone needed remedies they now relied on a woman and her daughter from Brading. The Bembridge Witch had by this time become a story to scare young children by the fireside at night. All except for Lucy Conway and Henry Thompson who still sorely missed her and the Moreys who felt strongly that they were still dealing with the effects of Molly Downer's curse upon their daughter. Harriet Morey had not uttered a word, or been able to move her limbs since the day that her grandmother had sent her money for her wedding, the wedding that had never taken place. Her mother shook her head in disgust, as she thought of the feckless William Gould. He had kept faith with his future wife for a whole fortnight, before he'd decided that if she wasn't likely to make a recovery, he was too young to spend his life tied to a girl locked in her own world and unable to communicate with anyone. He wanted to be a husband, not a carer and he'd packed all of his belongings one night without saying a word and disappeared. When they had sent Harriet's father to find him, his family had made their apologies and explained that he'd decided to travel to Portsmouth to find work and start afresh. Holding a cup to her daughter's lips, she tenderly wiped Harriet's face, as the water dribbled slowly down her chin. "There you go my love" she smiled. "I shall go and make you some stew, you like that don't you ? You just sit there and get well." She had said the same words for years, without so much as a slight improvement, but she still held a glimmer of hope that one day, she would have Harriet back to how she used to be, before that witch had ruined all their lives. The money that had been sent for the wedding had disappeared some time ago and caring for Harriet had been a financial burden, but one that they all felt was worth the sacrifice. The illness had struck her down so quickly that there had to be a chance that it would disappear just as quickly as it had arrived. Harriet's mother was busily chopping carrots, when she heard someone knock on the door. "Morning Mrs Morey." Turning around she saw the postman waiting at the door with a letter in his hand. She knew him from seeing him in the chapel, but the Moreys received post so infrequently that she was shocked to see him on her own doorstep. "Would you like a drink Daniel ?" She asked cheerfully.

"I'm sorry Mrs Morey but I have a heavy bag of post that I need to deliver." He declined, handing her the letter, which she saw was addressed to Harriet. "I wonder who could be writing to my daughter ?" She asked, as Daniel shrugged his shoulders and stood waiting, as she opened the envelope. As she pulled out the handwritten note inside, a twenty pound note fell onto the floor at her feet. Daniel stooped to pick it up and handed it to her. "What does it say?" He asked, intrigued at Mrs Moreys good fortune. "It is to do with Harriet's great aunt in Sandown, we haven't seen her in some time, she's been suffering from ill health, but she was particularly close to my Harriet, when she was a young girl. It says that when she died, she left this money in her will to Harriet." Turning away from Daniel, Mrs Morey took the money over to Harriet to show her. "Look my darling" she said. "Your great aunt has left you twenty pounds. It's quite a sum Harriet, she must have really loved you." As she took Harriet's hand to place the money in it, she noticed that her hands were unnaturally cold for such a warm day. "Harriet?" She asked, her voice taking on an urgent shrill tone. "Harriet." Her daughter looked as though she were asleep, but as she shook her shoulder, Harriet's head lolled on one side. "Mrs Morey" said Daniel gently, "Mrs Morey, she's gone."

"No she can't be" she screamed, shaking her head in denial. "This is a happy day, how can she die, the minute that she's been given the most money she's ever had in her life? How can she not be allowed to enjoy it?" Putting her hand to her mouth in horror, she realised what she'd said and what the obvious answer was, the curse of Molly Downer had worked. Her daughter had died before she was able to enjoy her good fortune, just as the witch had promised.

A Note from the Author about Molly Downer

The first time that I ever heard the story of Molly Downer, the 'Witch of Bembridge,' I was hooked. Molly was a ball of contradictions and I felt deeply that her story needed to be told, even though I resisted writing it for several years. Information on Molly is complex and although I have researched this story thoroughly and stayed true to the facts as far as possible, there were times when a reasoned judgement had to be made on what was the truth, also any historical inaccuracies are completely all my own. For instance, different sources document that Edward Wise, donated thirteen thousand pounds for the sum of the new chapel, whilst others claim it was one hundred pounds.

So let us first deal with what is the truth. Molly Downer was considered a witch by the people of Bembridge and they did want her tried, but were unsuccessful. She was the illegitimate daughter of the Reverend Jonathan Barwis of Niton, who left her a pittance when he died, despite being a man of some considerable means. She was well known to be a healer of minor illnesses and even the local schoolmaster praised her healing services. She was God fearing and reputed to be a handsome woman, alluring and attracted to men, though she never found a serious suitor. She did have a falling out with her best friend, with whom she had previously been inseparable. Some say this was because her friend got married and others believe it was over her friend's affair with a married man (though the names have been imagined for the purposes of this book.) She did publicly curse a villager named Harriet, with whom she had a long standing feud, stating 'should any good fortune fall upon her, she would die before possession.' Harriet died, three years after Molly and was said to have never regained the use of her limbs or speech after being cursed. It is also recorded that Harriet had received a letter notifying her that she had been bequeathed £20, Harriet died that same day...

Molly did become a recluse, who did not clean her house and villagers began to seriously believe that she was a witch, due to claims that she had poppets and bottles of liquids hanging in her window. Locals were annoyed at the time that the trials of witches had recently stopped. It is thought that she may have suffered from Diogenes Syndrome and her squalor was a result of illness, it is also conceivable that following the death of her father and mother and the incident with Harriet, could have plunged her into a deep depression. She was said to have charmed the smugglers to get free brandy, but I could not reconcile this with the God fearing woman she was said to be, so I have imagined here that she was connected with them for the purposes of financial benefit.

When she died, she did leave her belongings in her will to the vicar of the local church, with whom she had struck up an unlikely friendship, when he took pity on her, which had incensed the villagers. It is believed in some quarters, that this benevolence deeply embarrassed the reverend. The basis of their relationship is not fully known. Molly's father was not actually the first incumbent of the Chapel of Ease in Bembridge, it was a man named Sir Henry Thompson Baronet. Henry retired in 1836 and the next incumbent was Fred Middleton, who was still in his position at the time of Molly's death, so I have changed this for the purposes of the book. Molly was found by one of the charitable ladies who'd been leaving her religious texts in a cavity in her wall whilst other village ladies took the money she left out for them and left her provisions on a broken stool outside of her house. Molly was found lying dead in the back room of her home. The doors and windows of the cottage were all locked and her clothes were unruffled, her hands were serenely crossed and her eyes and mouths closed in peaceful repose. It was said that the villagers stripped, then re-clothed the body, after failing to find upon her the mark of a witch. They were then reported to have ransacked the house looking for money and the cottage was said to have been set alight and burned to the ground and is widely believed to have been rebuilt and named Myrtle Cottage, though there are those who believe that the house was not burnt, but was actually sold in the 1880s. Molly still lies in St Mary's Churchyard in Brading, but no one knows where her headstone is, it is believed to have been stolen in the 1960s, though it is still a matter of some debate whether she had a stone at all.

I have used truth and considered assumptions to weave the story of Molly's life, as closely as I possibly could and faithful to what facts remain over 170 years later. I hope you've enjoyed the book and find Molly Downer, as intriguing as I have.

Sarah

Made in the USA
Charleston, SC
20 August 2015